王無邪
Wucius Wong

王無邪
Wucius Wong

Published on the occasion of Spirit Of Sky And Land-Wucius Wong, organised by iPRECIATION

Published, designed and edited by
iPRECIATION
T : (65) 6339 0678
F : (65) 6438 2080
1 FULLERTON SQUARE, #01-08
SINGAPORE 049178
IPRECIATION.COM

ISBN: 978-981-08-1308-6
Cover: Partial of Sky And Land Expression #5

CONTENTS

目錄

Preface *by Helina Chan*	01	序言 *陳淑娟*
Artist's Own Words *by Wucius Wong*	03	畫家自述 *王無邪*
Plates	09	圖版
Biography	65	傳略
Index Of Works	68	作品索引

Preface

Helina Chan

Wucius Wong was born in 1936 in Guangdong Province, China. He moved to Hong Kong at very young age. He started as a self taught artist attracted to Western modernism. While experimenting, he acquired traditional Chinese painting techniques into his artform. He later studied under the tutelage of Lui Shou-kun who's work exploring traditional concept in a modernist approach. With his strong determination, he went to study the Western art in United States from 1961 to 1965.

The abstract art of Wucius Wong has a "powerful, mysterious quality"[1], being at once vigorously captivating and elusively atmospheric. Often compared to the classical Chinese landscape painters of the Northern Song dynasty, the artist has mastered the ability to evoke the deeply spiritual and poetic within his sweeping ink works. The emotions rendered by his brush span a wide range; from the luminous evanescence of the interplay of light on water, to the brooding gravity of mountain ranges, and the dense complexity of patternistic clouds and roots.

His formal composition and meticulous use of lines reveal his attraction to Western modernism, suggesting the organic yet structured depth of artists such as Jackson Pollock. This is apparent especially in the almost geometric organisation of works like *Spreading the Roots #3*. However his instinctive understanding of the propensities of white space and use of shifting visual perspectives show a fundamental desire to adhere to the principle of Chinese classicism in perpetuation of its three thousand year old lineage.

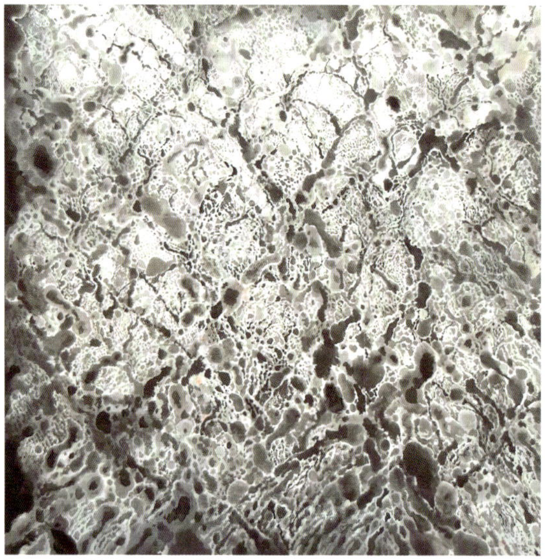

Spreading The Roots #3, 展根之三
Ink,Watercolour and Acrylic on Paper, 80 x 81 cm, 2007

While Wucius Wong rarely employs colour, preferring to retain the purity of the traditional ink and wash monochromes, in certain paintings such as *Spreading the Roots #7* and *Autumn River*, specks of colour are used to give a granular texture and enhance the movement of light across the surface of the work. This juxtaposition is all the more effective for his restraint – the colours are minimal and barely visible against the stark background and heavy contrasts of black and white.

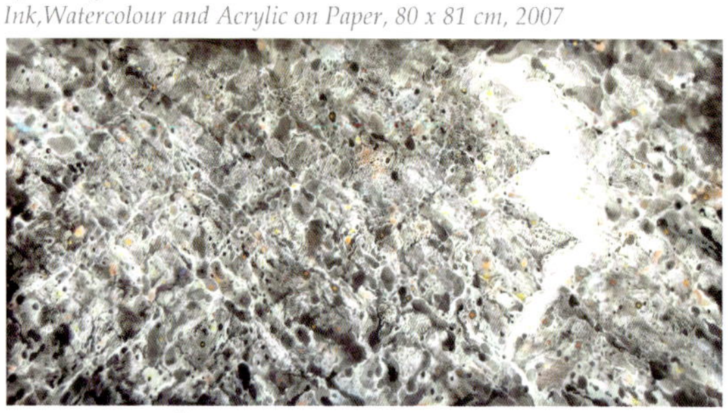

Autumn River, 秋江
Ink,Watercolour and Acrylic on Paper, 68.5 x 138.5 cm, 2008

At other times, his works have the meditative spontaneity of the great monk painters of the Qing Dynasty. The free flowing, limpid quality *The Edge of the Sea #2*, and its layered washes of ink bring to mind the works of Bada Shanren in particular, which appear to have been painted within a single introspective breath.

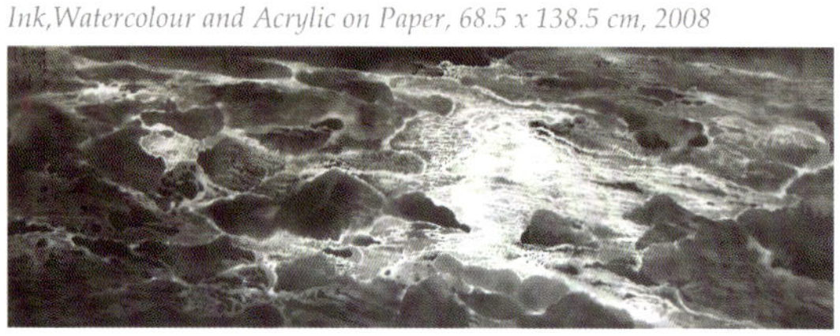

Edge Of Sea #2, 海緣之二
Ink,Watercolour and Acrylic on Paper, 30.5 x 94.5 cm, 2008

His critically acclaimed "Meditation" series of paintings continue to evolve in the creation of new forms and use of space and light, while retaining an almost mystical reverence for the sanctity of nature in its finest moments. This respect for the magnificent, yet austere aspects of soaring mountains and rushing waterfalls illustrates

序言

陳淑娟

王無邪1936年出生於中國廣東省，幼年移居香港。自習繪畫，受西方現代主義影響。在摸索過程中，想以國畫技法融入自己的藝術中，遂投入當時倡導新水墨路線之呂壽琨門下，更遠渡重洋，於1961至1965年間在美國修習西方藝術。

王無邪的畫作，富抽象感，具備一種"強勁而神秘的特性"[1]，既有引人入勝的強大魅力，又有一份難以捉摸的空靈氤氳。畫家常被人比擬為北宋古典山水名家， 懂得在奇恣縱橫的筆墨中觸動纏綿詩意、幽玄神思。他筆下演繹的情感紛紜多變；水光明滅、山巒沉鬱、老根盤錯、空中浮雲的文理繁密，俱有所陳。

他重視形式的構圖、線條的一絲不苟，無不顯露他的西方現代主義傾向，而且與某些藝術家（如美國的波洛克）講究結構的有機深度遙相呼應。這一點，在諸如《展根之三》等畫作近乎幾何式的組織方式中，尤其明顯。然而，畫家卻又在直覺上掌握了留白的特點，並且採用散點透視，顯示他在根本上其實渴望遵循中國古典技藝的原則，延續它已橫跨三千年的命脈。

王無邪雖然比較喜歡保留傳統單色水墨畫的純粹性，甚少著色，但在某些作品（如《展根之七》和《秋江》）中還是加入了點點色彩，以營造粒狀表面的質感及加強光線橫掃畫面之上的效果。正因為畫家的自我克制，這樣的並置安排反而更為有效－於此虛實鮮明的背景、反差強烈的黑白之中，彩色用量極少，幾乎肉眼難見。

王無邪的傑作，有時帶有清代偉大畫僧澄心入定、隨性自如的筆意。比如《海緣之二》的流暢通達、層層渲染，就讓人聯想到八大山人那些看似冥心觀照、一氣呵成的作品。

他備受好評的《澄懷》繪畫系列持續演變；畫家於此不僅創出各

the philosophical ethos of the artist, imbuing his works with an empathic nostalgia.

Perhaps the most affecting element within the paintings of Wucius Wong is his startling clarity in capturing fleeting moments within nature which have the ability to transcend the purely physical and translate into raw emotion. This unique perception is the defining factor which elevates hiswork from the realm of the visible landscape to incisive psychological meditations on existential humanity.

He is now an Adjunct Professor of the Fine Arts Department of the Chinese University of Hong Kong, and serving as honorary adviser to the Leisure and Culture Department of the Hong Kong Government, he is also Committee Member of the Art School of the Hong Kong Art Centre and a Member of the Museum Advisory Group of the Cosultative Committee on the Core Arts and Cultural Facilities of the West Kowloon Cultural District.

This exhibition showcases his works from 2003 to 2008.

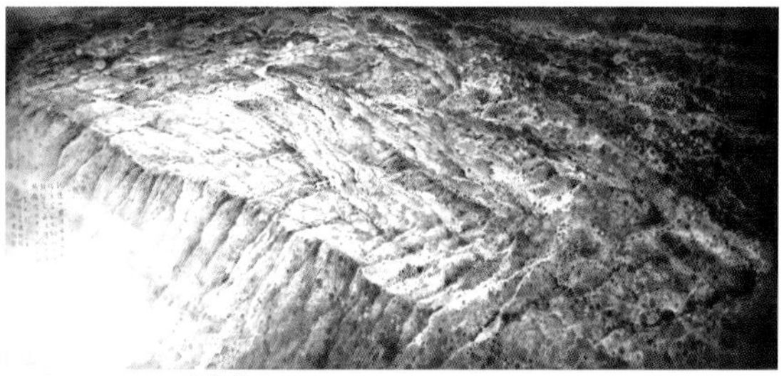

Meditation #26, 澄懷廿六
Ink,Watercolour and Acrylic on Paper, 96.5 x 212 cm, 2008

種新形態、巧用空間與光線，還保持了幾乎有些神秘主義意味的崇敬之意，禮讚神聖的天地大美。對崇山飛瀑的壯麗與嚴峻維持這種姿態，正好說明畫家的思想意境，也賦予作品精神磁性，使人心生同感，隨之懷念山水。

王無邪畫作中最具感染力的元素，或許是他捕捉大自然一瞬光輝時堪稱驚人的清晰度。這光輝一瞬，能超越純粹物質性的層次，實現轉化，凝聚出赤裸裸的情感來。畫家對此獨具慧眼，是決定性的因素；他的作品因而得以從肉眼所見的山水往上提升，透射出深刻的冥思，觀照作為一種存在的人性本質。

王無邪目前是香港中文大學藝術系的兼任教授、香港政府康樂文化署名譽顧問，同時也是香港藝術學院督導委員會成員、並且擔任西九龍文化區核心文化藝術設施諮詢委員會的博物館小組委員。

本展覽展示他2003至2008年的作品。

[1] *<Twentieth Century Chinese Painting>: James Cahill and Maychingg Kao*

[1]《二十世紀中國繪畫》：高美慶編，詹姆斯·卡希爾等人撰文。

Artist's Own Words

by Wucius Wong

THE SPIRIT OF SKY AND LAND

My work aims to capture the spirit of sky and land which fully occupies my heart, fills my eyes, and invigorates my brush.

At a glance, some of my work may look abstract. Actually representational elements are always there, and they are usually related to the Chinese tradition. As most Chinese landscape paintings leave the sky blank, I love to fill it with clouds and mist without clearly defining the horizon. My recent work aims to show the sky and land to express the immensity of space beyond ordinary landscapes.

Sky and land can open up thousands of miles in space, and stretch beyond a fixed moment in time. The Tang poet Du Fu once exclaimed: "The River Jin tints the sky and land with Spring colours as the Yulei Mountains spread clouds to signify change of the times." What is seen may be the same as what is felt, but what is felt supersedes what is seen.

Literary critic Liu Xie (active around 4th Century) also wrote: "Feelings fill the mountain as one ascends the mountain, and thoughts flood the sea as one gazes at the sea." In an act of empathy, the artist becomes the mountain and sea, or the sky and land, which have been created with his brush.

Clouds as Feelings and Water as Thoughts

The sky above us is filled with the atmosphere. The atmosphere contains water vapour that accumulates as fluffy cloud masses, thins down as mist and fog, and becomes rain, snow, or ground water with condensation. Clouds are visible substance mediating between the sky and land. They float, gather, or disperse, seemingly immaterial.

Land is under our feet, stretching laterally in all directions. It rises as mountains, sinks as valleys, protrudes as ridges, soars as peaks, drops as slopes, and plunges as cliffs. Water on the land surface would slide into the low lying areas. It meanders as streams and rivers, forms lakes when enclosed by land, and runs into the sea. Land can be veiled by clouds and mist.

Light illuminates the sky and land. The sun is the main light source. Sunlight is bright on fine days, but gets diffused on overcast days. Everything visible to our naked eyes with the presence of light which comes in a definite direction but can be bounced back, reflected, refracted, or filtered. Shade is there when light weakens or is blocked. Light and shade together can accomplish visual drama in a painting, along with clouds activating movement and water bringing in life.

These constantly changing elements make up the main vocabulary in my work. Clouds hover aimlessly. Water flows with no return. Light captures a fleeting event in time and space. All these can have emotional impact. Living in seclusion abroad, I frequently painted the river to represent the feeling of drifting away from the homeland.

Our hearts would tremble with wind sweeping, clouds surging, water cascading, or light dimming, but would find tranquillity with mist spreading quietly and ripples surrounding the shore. Nature comes alive with clouds as breaths, water as blood, and light as spirit, all in perpetual

畫家自述

王無邪

天地情懷

獨與天地精神往來，天地在我心中，天地在我眼中，天地在我筆下。

我的作品乍眼看來，有時頗為抽象，實際上都有具象成分，多見傳統中國山水畫語彙。不過傳統山水畫常將天作為空白背景，我則喜歡以雲霞泛天，模糊化天地分界。天地也可作山水主題，但天地氣象比山水更大。

以天地為師，眼界有千尋萬里，胸中有古往今來，無窮盡的空間，無窮盡的時間。這就如杜甫登樓詩名句，「錦江春色來天地，玉壘浮雲變古今，」感慨超絕時空，景化為情，情勝於景。

劉勰在「文心雕龍」神思篇也說過，「登山則情滿於山，觀海則意溢於海，」情與意，比眼中的山水，尤為重要。畫家的心靈，向實景投射，筆下成山成水，為天為地，其實都代表畫家的自我。

雲情水意

天在上，以雲為形。雲是氣體，由水蒸氣構成，厚則成球，薄可成帶，散起成霞，稀可成霧，遇冷凝為雨或雪，着地或變水。雲飛于天，虛無縹緲，若實若虛，忽聚忽散。浮雲下飄，則與地相接。

地在下，是無邊界的實體。地之聳起，則凸而成山，凹而成谷，橫為嶺，尖為峰，斜為坡，峭為崖。地面有水，則積而為湖泊，瀉而為泉瀑，奔而為溪澗，流而為江河，儲而為海洋。雲掩地，則隱沒地之部分輪廓，水覆地，則因地而成形。

天地之間有光。一般由太陽來，晴天有強光普照，陰天也有柔光，令人肉眼可辨萬物。光本身無形，但有強弱，有方向，由上而下，或有側面斜射，令萬物具形。光影使畫面元素有隱有顯，產生戲劇性效果，加強感情表現。天地得雲而動，得水而活。得光而靈。

雲情水意，常是我畫面主要元素。雲水因光照耀，尤能變化萬千。雲出岫漂泊無定，水東流不能逆轉，光能成影，也代表光陰，呈達剎時的景象，引起某時某地某事的感嘆。我客居國外時，與河為鄰，多以江河谷壑作為繪畫主題，流露

melodic movements and rhythmic tempos, which can be expressed in a painting.

Creation of Form and Momentum

As basic elements in a painting, dots are linked together as lines, and lines are joined to enclose plane. A plane can be solid or open. Edge of a plane is perceived as a shape. A shape can be abstract if it makes no reference to the reality. An abstract shape can still convey emotion with its length and size, colour and shade, as well as texture and edge definition. Furthermore, there are also general shape characteristics, and the effects of brush and ink.

Planes can combine to create representational three-dimensional forms with illusory volume and depth, to be recognized as mountains, humans or anything in our day-to-day world. When reference to the reality is vague, they might provide hints and still serve to stimulate the viewer's imagination.

Painting the sky and land along with clouds and water, I would load my brush with wet ink, or stain it with sparing ink, and drag it freely across the paper surface to create representational forms, semi-abstract forms, or entirely abstract shapes, and let these work together to externalize inner feelings and thoughts. Traditional Chinese painting media are fittingly suitable in this way of expression.

As in calligraphy, a large or small brush with long or short, stiff or soft hair, can be used to generate a special directional force. It can be held vertically or in a slanting way, moved with the arm, the wrist, the hand, or just the fingers, with intermittent turns and bends, in slow or quick motion. There are different parts in a brush: the tip, the body, and the heel, with hair in a sharp point or disarranged, to produce special effects.

As in music, I can use the brush to trace a curling path similar to a letter C, or a winding path similar to a letter S, with the visible and half-hidden elements arranged in a linear movement. Long lines can represent to sounds of string instruments playing the main melodic theme, whereas dots and short lines can represent to piano sounds and percussions as echoes and consonance. Visual orchestration is achieved with lines and dots together.

As in design, forms occupying a surface bounded with four straight lines joined at right angles can display elements in random, parallel, or radiating directions, or inside grids. Their shapes can repeat or vary, and they can overlap, intersect or join one another, to attain a harmonious or stunning visual effect.

Multiple Backgrounds and Inclinations

Borrowing aesthetic principles in calligraphy, music and design reflects my multiple backgrounds and inclinations. With wide intellectual interest and taste for different art forms, I have identified four cornerstones: literature, design, the Chinese tradition, and Western modernism, on which my art is based, among other influences.

I loved literature during my formative years and wanted to pursue a literary career. I contributed poems and critical essays to numerous local

異地客情。

風起雲湧，水衝泉瀉，使人心弦震動，煙霧迷濛，清漣繞岸，引起幽深聯想。大自然充滿生機，永有抑揚頓挫的節奏，周而復始的韻律。雲水是畫的血脈，光是畫的精神。近作更注重筆勢表現，強化生生不息的動感。

建象取勢

積點成線，圍線得面，面有虛實，其邊緣輪廓，可辨為形。形無所似，則呈示全抽象的畫面，以筆觸之緩急、利鈍、長短、疏密、疊接、聚散，墨瀋之濃淡、乾濕、溜化，色彩之明暗、鮮晦、寒暖、清濁，作為形之本質，以動靜、巨細、繁簡、曲直、圓缺傳遞感情。

平面化的形，正側相合，構集成體。體有厚度，則幻成象。象有所似，則成具象而擬山、擬水、擬人、擬物，清晰重現日常的視覺世界。象又可在抽象與具象之間，易辨又不易辨，有體亦若無體，虛實互換，遠近交錯，引起觀者聯想。

我寫天地雲水，順筆成形，由形建象，不拘泥於似，也不拘泥於不似。形與象情景相生，意在筆先，情超象外，非實非幻，成畫面意境。醮墨運筆，勾線得面，構面呈體，皴擦作肌理，渲染顯光影，在我來說，中國傳統繪畫媒材則優為之。

用筆取勢反映傳統中國的書法美學。毛筆有大小之別；鋒毫有長短、軟硬之選，有輕重、緩急、正側、順逆之用。其不同部份，筆尖、筆肚、筆根、散毫，各有效果。指、腕、手、臂，驅毫取鋒，以提頓轉折、濃淡乾濕致趣。

筆勢產生動感，以乍顯乍隱的視覺元素，展出C形順行的捲勢，或S形反覆的扭勢，以多元伏線帶引觀者視線搜索畫面。這會與音樂美學有關。長線的延伸有如弦樂，帶領出主旋律，而以短線與大小的點，有如鋼琴、琵琶或敲擊樂，配上和音節奏，或作多調爭鳴。

畫面邊緣由四條直線以直角框成，可暗藏水平、垂直、傾斜方向，或組成十字、交叉、井字、斜格，將空間劃分。在另一方面，形之重複、近似、串列、旋轉、發射，面塊之聯接、疊集、虛實、對立、貫通，我會參用設計美學，以求視覺調協，或求打

newspapers and magazines, published a journal of poetry with friends, and established a literature and art association. Soon I understood the problems of developing as poet and writer in Hong Kong. With some natural drawing skills, I began to join local sketching tours and gradually shifted my aspirations to the pursuit of an artist's career.

I started as a self-taught artist attracted to Western modernism. While doing my own experimentation, I wanted to acquire traditional Chinese painting techniques at the same time. Thus I became a student of Lui Shou-kwan, whose work exploring traditional concepts in a modernist approach had my admiration. Under his guidance, I first copied a Dun Huang cave painting and a work by Bada Shanren, but I generally concentrated on the landscape paintings by Song masters.

This Chinese side was to be complemented with a Western side. I went to a private art academy in Hong Kong for drawing lessons but found the approach too old-fashioned for me. Determined to study Western art in the West, I was able to enrol in one art college for two years and another for two more years. As theories and concepts interested me more than practical techniques, I continued to pursue my own path in the traditional Chinese painting media.

Design to me is an attitude and a way of systematic thinking. I was particularly attracted to the basic principles on which I was able to accomplish my own interpretations. Application of some of such principles can actually help me to break away from the age-long tradition.

In the past fifty years, my painting style has evolved, but never consistently in one single direction. At different space and time, one of my multiple backgrounds might get greater emphasis. In most cases, I would find back to the tradition and march forward again in a new direction. There is always literature in my heart, but I discover design with my eyes. There is the Chinese tradition strengthening my bones, but my mind is often filled with Western modernism.

I would seek transcendentalism and lyricism as a poet, but do analytical thinking and orderly arrangement like a designer. I would paint in the traditional Chinese media in a contemporary Western approach, but occasionally would also paint with oil and acrylic colours on canvas, to resemble a Chinese painting. In any case, my attempt is to bridge East and West, or to make a complete crossover, only to establish something entirely mine.

Finding my Source and Spreading my Roots

Like a bird tired of flying, I came back to Hong Kong to eye-witness the handover and seek permanent stay. I have already found my source, and wish to spread my roots now. The skyscrapers in Hong Kong are much taller than older days, shielding most of the mountain behind. I began to include these in my work. As an inseparable part of China, Hong Kong should move on with new orientation.

The city is a place of high congestion, and offers little room for comfortable accommodation. Living on the mid-levels, I frequently painted the skyscrapers. Then I was particularly interested in the windows, openings and gaps, and sought to transform them into trees and rocks as appearing in daydreams, to express my yearnings for Nature. I am now residing

破常規，呈示嶄新美感。

多元背景

借鑑繪畫之外的其他美學，反映我成長的多元背景。我的起點是文學，曾從事設計教育工作，留學進修藝術之前已有中國書畫底子，在西方藝術學院獲得全面藝術基礎。所以我曾說過，我的繪畫建立於四種基石之上：文學、設計、中國傳統、和西方現代。

我早年喜歡文學，中學時代開始寫作，曾立志要成為詩人。中學畢業後出版過期刊，組織過會社，有新詩、散文、論文在報章、雜誌發表。不過我自幼受雙語教育，畢業於英文中學，自覺語文基礎薄弱，難成大器，遂轉向繪畫發展。

在繪畫方面，我接觸現代西方文學時已有接觸現代西方繪畫，初憑自學搜索，後追隨呂師壽琨學傳統中國畫法，同時也以水墨媒材放膽創新。我的臨摹範圍，上及敦煌，下探八大，而專注董源、巨然、郭熙、馬遠、夏圭諸家。

在學習水墨畫之前，我參加過美專夜校的素描課程，對舊式的教學不以為然。我認為應赴歐美進修西方藝術，結果成功申請得獎學金，在美國兩所不同的美術學院前後留了四年。西方現代藝術和設計理論，對我有較深刻的啟發。

設計既是造形和視覺文法，也是一種思考方式。在這方面我曾深入探討，在教學之外，寫過一些理論書籍，頗能一紙風行。我將平面設計的某些基本原則，應用在水墨畫上，在造形與構圖方面都有助突破傳統樊籬。

在長達五十年的藝術追尋中，經驗之遞增，環境之變易，使我產生不同的畫風，時地不同，多元背景偏重也異。我回歸東方，又朝新的方向出發，不過對中國傳統，始終有所堅持，常以文學為心，設計作眼，傳統建骨，現代創意而自勵。

我自己覺得，氣質近乎文人，嚮往空靈超脫，典雅幽邃，但又似設計家，偏愛分析思考，注重完美成果。我以水墨畫求現代感，又以油畫求水墨皴染效果，想獨闢蹊徑，不完全屬於東方，更不完全屬於西方，在邊界與邊界之間尋獲屬於我的空間，那是跨界的空間。

on the southern part of the island and can see the sea everyday. The sea has an infinite capacity for receiving water from rivers in every direction. I want to capture the magnificent force of the sky and land with boundless vision.

I still paint the mountains to represent my inner spirit as standing on top of the highest peak to look down on all other peaks, away from the hustling world. I still paint the river that flows down from the distant horizon, tracing back to the only source that I do not have to look for another. I frequently paint trees with their strong extending roots which are my own roots. I watch the infinite sky, recognizing that I am no longer the wanderer in the past.

The Hong Kong Museum of Art presented my large-scale retrospective from December 2006 till March 2007. In that exhibition, I divided my pursuit in five phases: Searching for Identity (1956-1964), Order and Expression (1965-1974), Tracing back to the Source (1975-1984), Seclusion and Contemplation (1985-1995), and Looking for Roots - Building a Dream (1996-2006). The exhibition, entitled "At the East-West Crossroads," revealed my crossover pursuit over half a century. In the latest phase, some of the works on display showed the use of bold brush in an expressive manner. Most of works in the present exhibition emphasize this tendency, which means that I have entered the sixth phase in my development.

With the sky and land in my heart, I think I have gained greater freedom with the brush at this time in search of an immensely broad vision of the sky and land.

Wucius Wong

Early summer, 2008 , Hong Kong

認源展根

香港回歸後，我烏倦知還，在香港長居，認源展根。香港幢幢的高樓大廈，與山比高，不免成為一些作品的題材。不過我也感到香港與中國血脈相連，必須重新定位，建立新紀元氣象。所以我漸在畫面增強磅礡之勢。

城市是一種緊逼壓縮的空間，使我驚覺天地之大，不知棲身何處。我寫城市景物，會以建築門窗，幻化為樹，表現對大自然的渴望。近年遷居港島南郊，常見遼闊海面，所以也喜寫海，以海納八川，有容乃大，表達對宏大空間的憧憬。

我仍然會寫高聳的山，作為自己化身，一覽眾山小，遺世獨立，另拓自己天地。我仍然會寫江河，今日寫的則是由天上來的江河，而我已無須再盲目尋源。我間而寫樹，尤喜寫根，因為再無失根之痛。極目天涯，但我不在天涯，今日已非遊子。

二〇〇六年底至二〇〇七年初，香港藝術館主辦了我的大型回顧展，五十年的藝術追尋分作五階段：展步立我，構理顯情，溯源覓流，遠隱反思，及尋根建夢。回顧展的主題為「東西問道」，其中的第五階段已見意筆縱橫。我覺得目前此次在新加坡展出的大部分作品，都顯示我已踏入第六階段。

天地情懷，是此新階段的重點，我希望能以筆墨開闢比山水更恢宏的畫境。

王無邪

二〇〇八年初夏香港

NEITHER CHINESE NOR WESTERN

I rarely feel fully satisfied with what I have already accomplished. I am in constant search of new, unexplored avenues, considering further attempts from a broad perspective. Confident at times, I sometimes get frustrated in overcoming hindrances. I am fond of experimenting with a wide range media and pursuing different stylistic expressions simultaneously. Water and ink have been my most favorable media. Switching to oil and acrylic paint on canvas, I would seek water and ink effects. My concerns are whether the development of ink painting has reached a dead end, and whether ink painting could acquire new vigour.

Since the autumn of 1999, I have been teaching on a course entitled "Modern Ink Painting" at the Fine Arts Department of the Chinese University of Hong Kong. Students are mostly from the graduating year of the department, whose chosen majors range from Chinese painting, Chinese calligraphy, Western painting, sculpture, printmaking, to multi-media. There are also students from other departments. Distinctions between Chinese painting, ink painting, and modern ink painting, cultural identity of Hong Kong artists, and status of contemporary Chinese artists in the international art world, are issues that frequently occur in my mind.

Artistic creation marks a long unending path. I have played multiple roles in the Hong Kong art scene since the end of the Second World War, with activities in art mixed with diverse interests and involvement in literature, design, criticism and education. In my observation, Hong Kong art, particularly in the area of painting media, show little progress in recent years, although after the handover, Hong Kong artists have attained greater international exposure. Can Painting as an art form still adequately express the complicated phenomena of the new century? There is no doubt, however, that painting, achievable single-handedly by anyone beyond the restriction of space and time, should never fall into obsolescence.

In the West, painting only refers to work achieved with oil or acrylic paint on canvas or board, and ink painting could be easily regarded as drawing or watercolor. The emergence of China as an economic power exerting greater influence in international affairs, we can expect that ink painting will gain proper recognition in the general painting category, and will be practiced also by artists of non-Chinese descent. What exactly makes an ink painting? The Chinese characters shui, mo, and hua, forming the term point to the presence of water and ink. A more conservative point of view demands the use of brush and ink in an ink painting to conform to standards established by the early masters, and to express elevated spirits of the heart. Traditionally, painting and calligraphy share the same foundation, and elevated spirits reflect the taste of the literati who were trained in ancient classics.

Today, professionals of different disciplines have completely replaced the literati who occupied the upper sector of the society. As China faces challenge of the Western civilization and seeks modernization, most of the older values are undergoing revision. In the early Twentieth Century, many Chinese artists practicing ink painting strove to make significant diversion from the tradition by integrating lessons from classical and modern Western art.

不問中西

我一向不以目前的創立感到滿足，常想搜索尚未墾闢的道路。我從宏觀角度思考個人藝術的進取，有時充滿信念，但又有時覺得力不從心。我在同一期間，往往作多線式的探索，不同媒介與風格的實驗。我較傾向使用水墨媒介，寫油畫也希求水墨效果。目前的挑戰是，水墨畫已否抵達了山窮水盡的地步，抑或可以轉化而獲得新的動力？

什麼是“中國畫”，什麼是“水墨畫”，什麼是“現代水墨畫”，這些詞語之定義，香港藝術家之身分認同，當代中國藝術家之定位，都是間歇盤旋腦際的問題。藝術創作是一條悠長的道路。文學、設計、評論、教育，曾是我創作之外的興趣，佔去我不少時間。第二次世界大戰後香港藝術的發展，我扮演過不同的角式，包括藝術課程策劃及美術館行政工作。

繪畫能否表現複雜的二十一世紀社會生活，是一個爭議性問題，但作為個人可以單獨完成的、不受預設空間和時間限制的一種創作表現，應不易為其他藝術形式取代的。水墨畫是繪畫類別之一，雖然一般所謂繪畫，是指油彩或丙烯彩施在布上的平面作品。不過隨著中國經濟之急劇起飛，中國在國際舞台上漸擔任舉足輕重的角式，水墨畫成為受國際藝壇認許的畫種，水墨為中國以外地區的藝術家樂用的媒介，機會很大。

什麼是水墨畫？嚴格來說，從媒介的角度，水墨畫是有水有墨。更嚴格些來說，從中國人一般較保守的立場，水墨畫上承逾千年的中國繪畫傳統，不僅要有水有墨，還得用筆有方，用墨有法，并顯現典雅情懷。筆墨方法，須具深厚書法基礎；典雅情懷，必以文人品味為依歸。

古代學而優則仕的文人早已消失，代之而興的是不同行業的專業人士。社會的轉型改變了舊有的價值觀念，中國文化面對西方挑戰，逾百年來，不斷尋求現代化的出路。二十世紀不少中國畫家，接受西方繪畫的影響，尤在古典寫實方面，初建水墨畫的新貌。

在八〇年代以前，中國藝壇一直以中國畫或水墨畫為主流，而實驗性的水墨畫，亦即現代水墨畫，遲至九〇年代，方在大陸冒起，成為一股令人矚目的新生力量。不過同期的中國油畫，也有可觀的發展。我們很難說未來的中國繪畫，那種媒介形式，會

In Hong Kong around the late nineteen fifties, under the influence of postwar Western art, development of ink painting found a new turn. The "modernist ink painting" movement began to make an impact on the art scene. Parallel developments were seen also in Taiwan and overseas around the same time or slightly later. The characteristics of modern ink painting have not yet been clearly defined, for each artist, curator, art historian, or art critic, has an individual view.

Ink painting seemed to dominate the Chinese art scene up to the nineteen-eighties. Works identifiable as modern ink painting did not appear to stir the art scene until the nineteen-nineties, at a time when contemporary Chinese art showed considerable emancipation. In this new century, it is hard to predict which art form will eventually lead in China. Needless to say, oil painting has a Western origin, and Chinese artists still have plenty to learn from the West; ink painting has obvious Eastern roots. It can now be certain that the tradition of Chinese painting has not been completely destroyed by the aggressively spreading Western civilization. A new foundation for Chinese culture is to be built with pluralistic efforts. Each Chinese artist can find an individual way as determined by background training, personal taste and preferences, ability and aspirations, to revitalize or transform the tradition, and make a contribution.

Can Hong Kong artists also contribute positively to this foundation? Under the British rule, we were brought up in a bilingual environment, and our understanding of the Chinese or the Western culture was generally shallow. The shallowness, however, provides us greater capacity in receiving new ideas. The weakness is actually a kind of strength. Our pursuit in art has been inevitably based on the intermixture of Chinese and Western culture.

Who am I? What have I done? What do I want to do? What should I do? What can I do? What more can I do? Such are questions that prompt for answers from every artist. I have at one time advocated that we should all find back to our Eastern source and subsequently move away from it to explore new directions. Now I realize that East and West are all within us, and our blood vessels contain the Eastern cells, as well as some Western cells.

To establish the strength as a Hong Kong artist, one need not make a distinction between what is Chinese and what is Western. We create ink painting with water and ink, but can we do it without water and ink? What expresses the spirit of water and ink is probably the most important. Are we able to simulate water and ink effects, and attempt to make lines and marks without the traditional Chinese brush? Conversely, can we use the Chinese brush to make lines and marks as if they were obtained with unorthodox methods? There should be no boundary separating paint media, art forms, and cultural expressions.

Wucius Wong

2002

佔領導地位。不過油畫畢竟是西方產物，中國人學習油畫，總要向西方取經，而水墨畫無論如何西化，畢竟具有東方的根源。

可以肯定的是，中國的繪畫傳統，在強勢的西方文化衝擊之下，沒有完全潰散。每一創作者都會根據其背景、師承、偏愛、能力、品味、抱負，選定個人的方向，偏向維護傳統，或破舊立新。其能力之所及，意願之所寄，機緣之所許，在誠心盡力下，必有所成，奠下中國建立新文化新藝術多元多極的基礎。

我是誰？我曾做過什麼？我想做什麼？我應做什麼？我能做什麼？我還能做什麼？每一藝術創作者，都要為這些問題提出答案。我曾主張回到東方再出發，其實東方的血球，就在體內脈絡之中，但脈絡內也包括一些西方的血球。

不問中西，不存成見，不拒斥新的事物、新的觀念，有容乃大。創作水墨畫，是水是墨，似水似墨，似筆非筆，似寫非寫，似印非印，似紙非紙，從而跨媒介、跨形式、跨文化，有何不可？

王無邪

二〇〇二

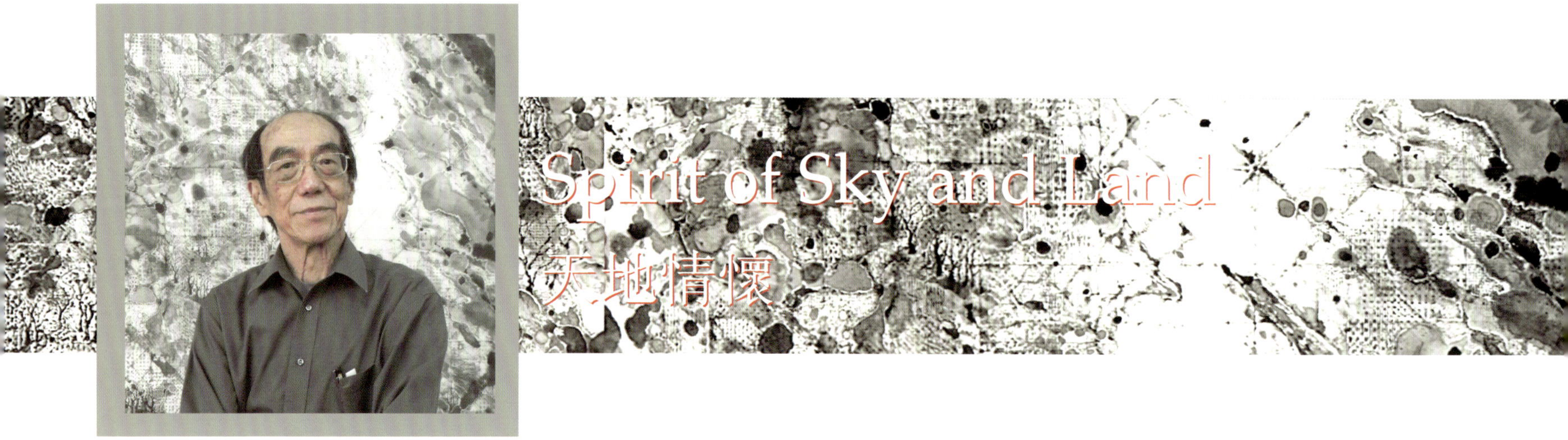

Spirit of Sky and Land
天地情懷

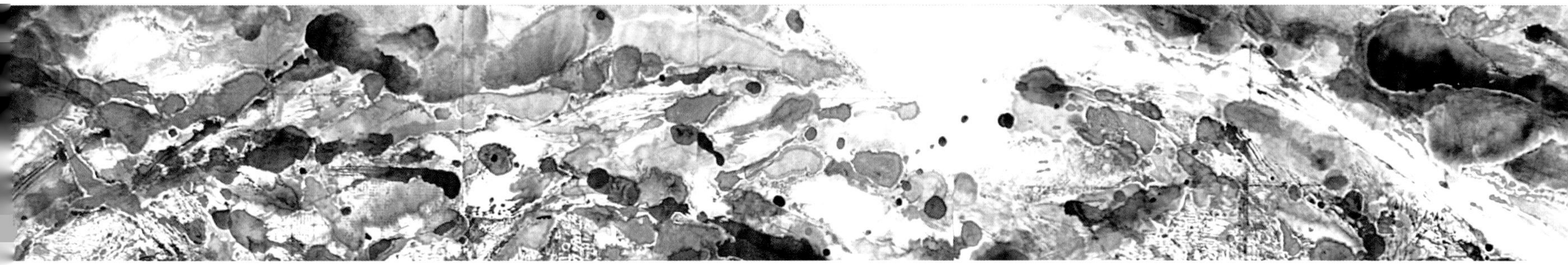

My work aims to capture the spirit of sky and land which fully occupies my heart, fills my eyes, and invigorates my brush.
獨與天地精神往來，天地在我心中，天地在我眼中，天地在我筆下。

Partial of Dream City #12
城夢十二局部

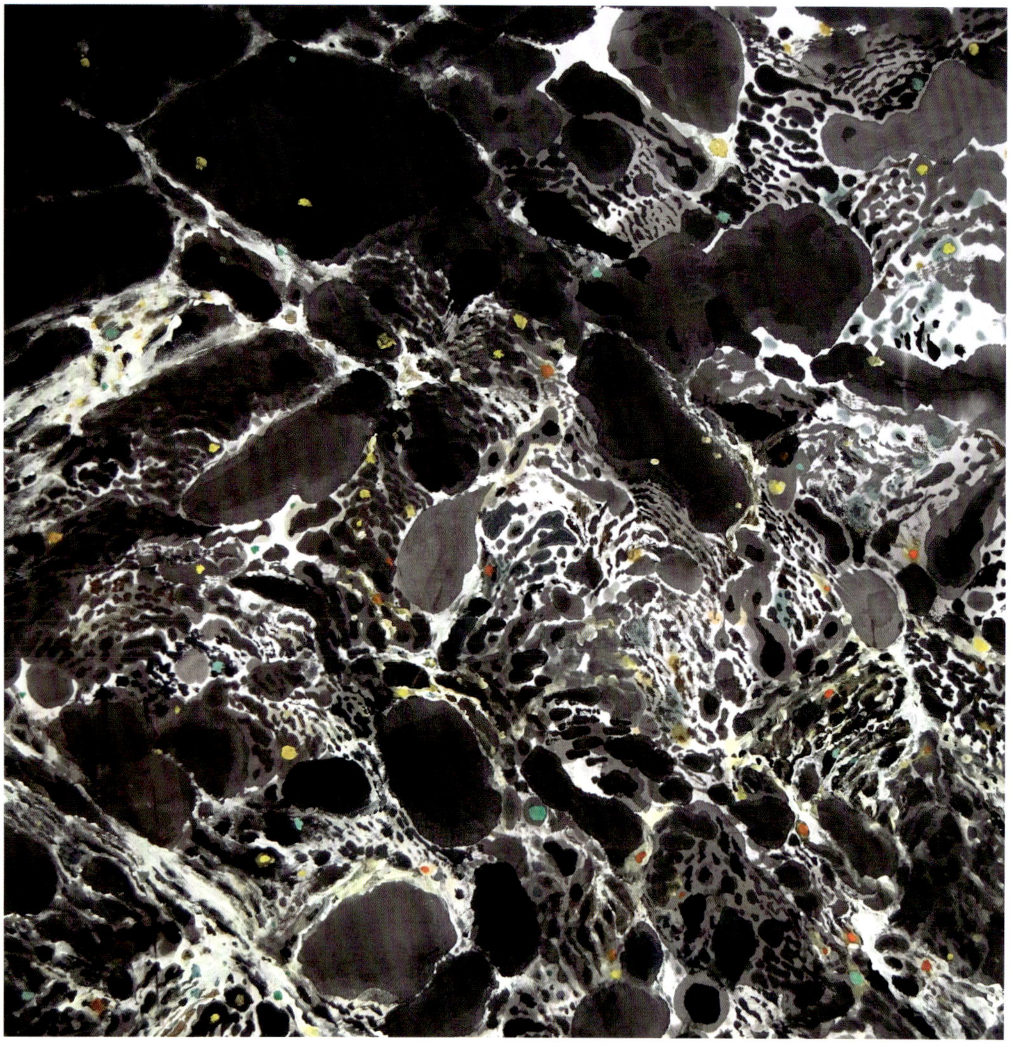

Partial detail of the top left

局部細節(左上)

This painting is on cotton fabric mounted as a pair of scrolls to form a diptych, portraying sky and clouds, land and water, intermingled in perpetual orchestration. It expresses an ultimate communion with Nature, which exists beyond existence, and moves beyond movement.

此作寫在棉布上，裱為一對相連立軸，表現天、雲、地、水互相交織的畫面。各種元素混成一體，產生一種永恆的動感。天地與我並生，萬物與我為一，存于空間之外，動超時間之外，生生不息，成為周而復始的韻律，在永恆的交響中。

Sky And Land Expression #5

天地情之五(二連屏)

Ink,Watercolour and Acrylic on Cotton Fabric

200 x 200 cm [Diptych], 2008

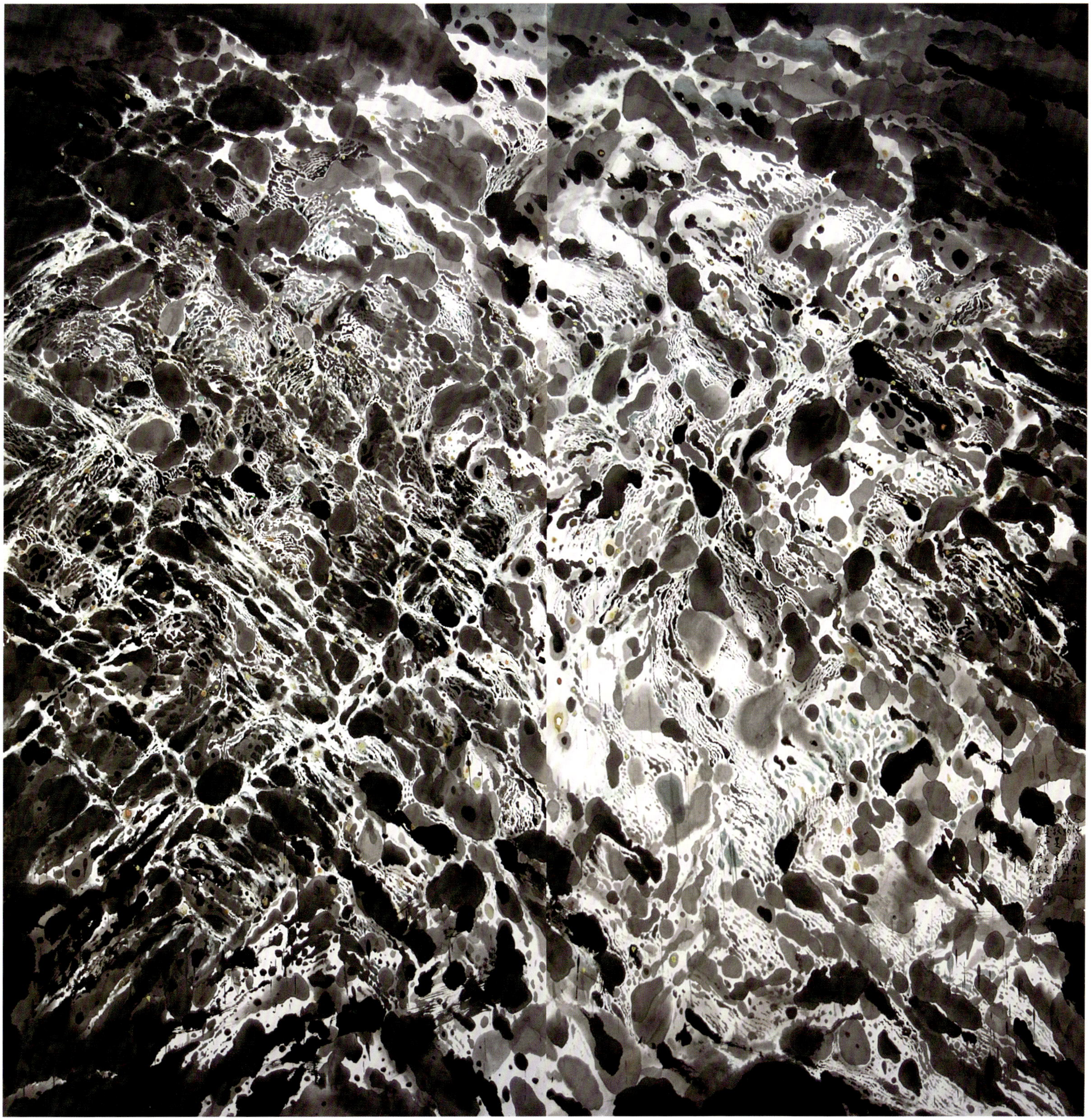

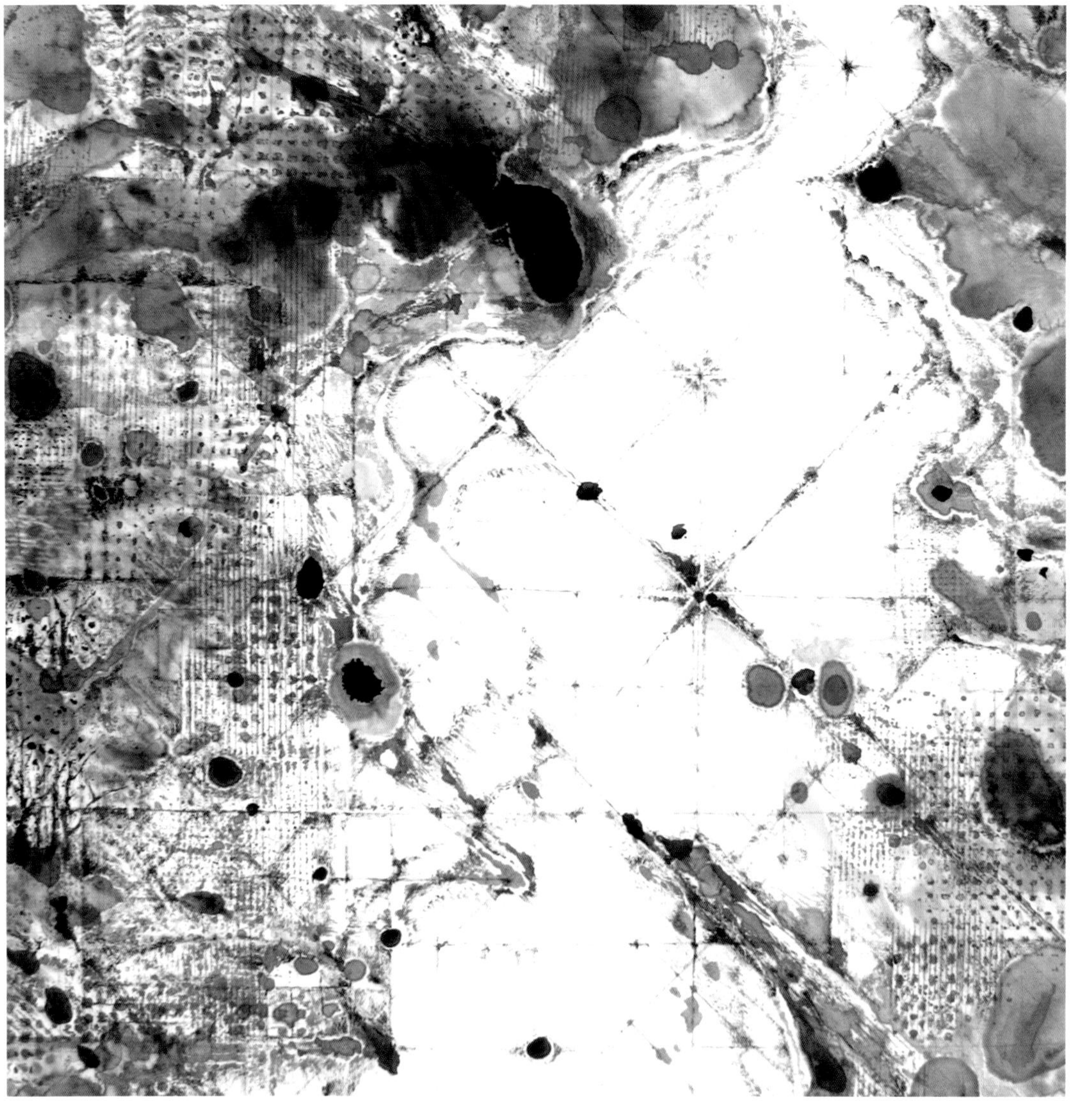

Broad daylight will come and night will end
City dwellers will face another bustling day
They enter and leave the skyscrapers
Jamming into congestion and polluted air
Bombarded with noises and electronic waves
Away from green lawns and lucid water
In the absence of blue sky and white clouds
Where can rhythms of Nature be found
Not before our eyes probably in our dreams

黎明始終要來　睡夢會結束
城中人面臨另一繁忙的日子
從高廈出來　進入另一幢高廈
在擠逼環境中　污濁空氣中
受到噪音與電波不斷侵擾
難再見綠草如茵　碧水長流
藍天白雲早成為稀有景象
大自然有生生不息的韻律
不在眼中　也許在心中夢中

Partial detail of the right
局部細節（右）

City Dream #12
城夢十二（二連屏）
Ink,Watercolour and Acrylic on Paper
176 x 190 cm [Diptych], 2004

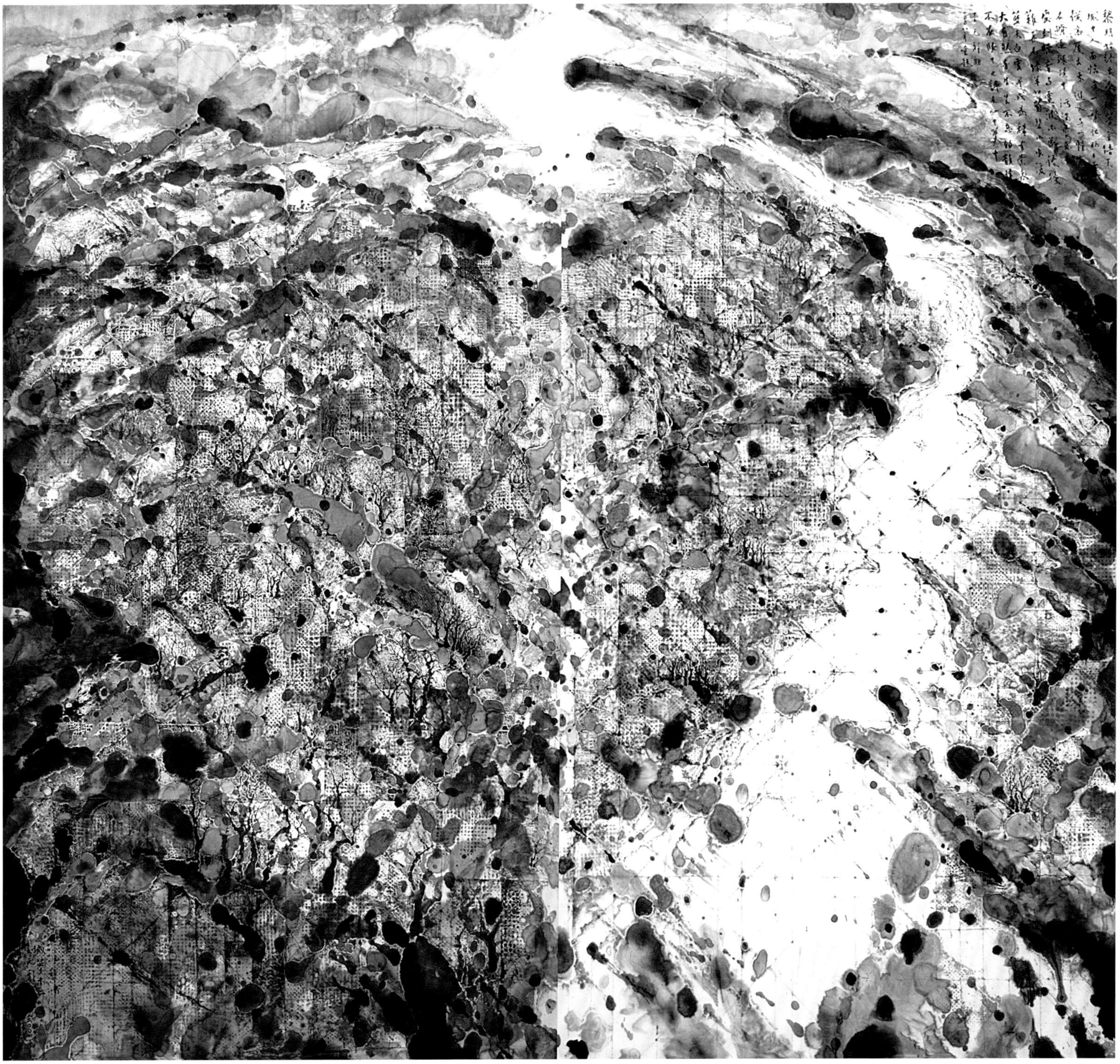

This diptych portraits the city, with mountain and harbour, activated by a circulating movement of the rhythms of Nature. After a hardworking day, can we all escape into the dreams?

此連屏呈示城市的山和海港，旋動於大自然的韻律中。我們日出而作，能否日入而息，尋向夢中，一洗日間的辛勞？

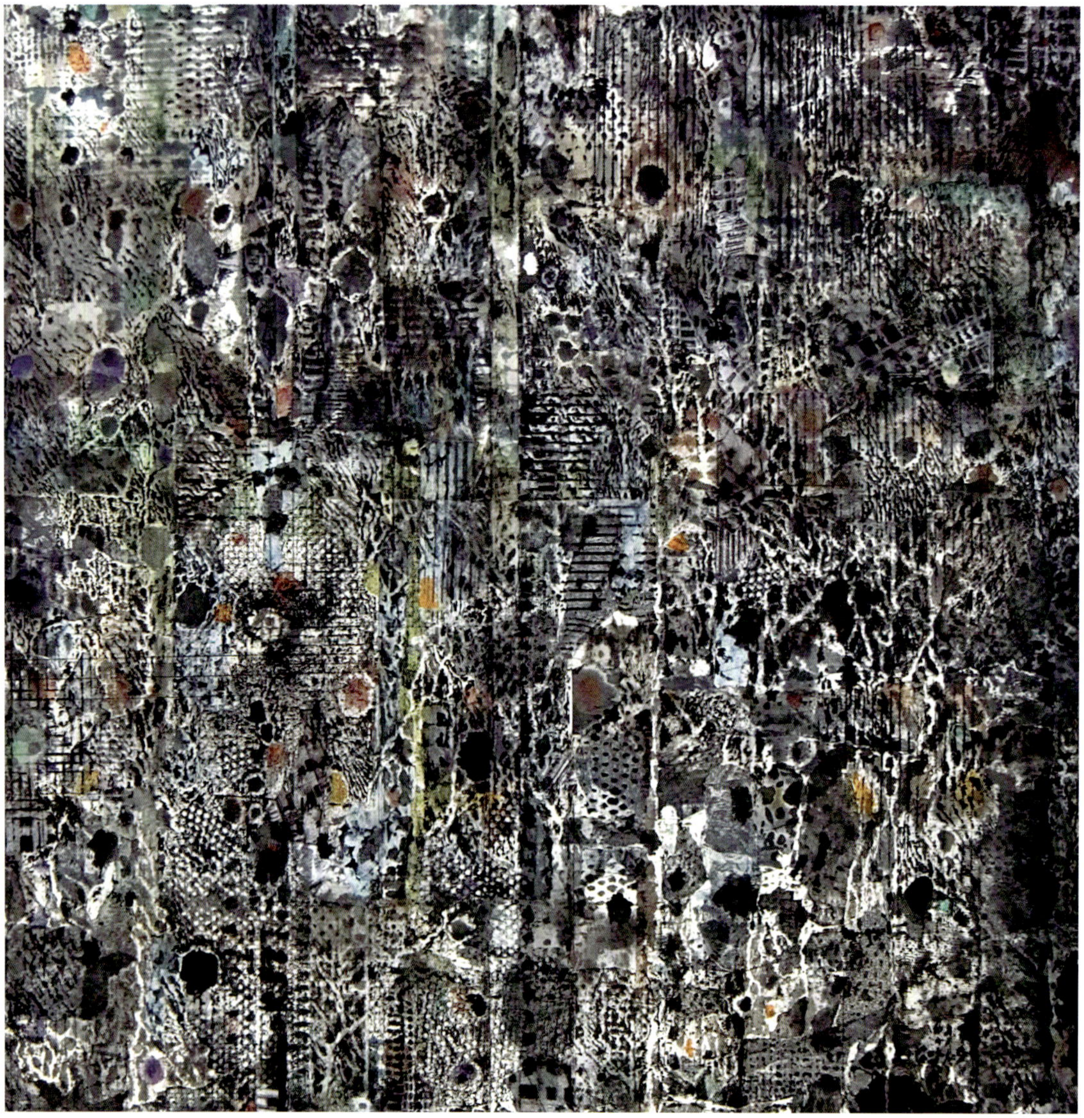

Partial detail of the central

局部細節（中）

In which year and which month
At what hour and what minute
With the heart containing this city
And this city containing this dream
We woke up in nowhere
And we found no place to live
What was seen was never seen
What was known was never known
Dots and lines fill the space
Seemingly real yet unreal
What was solid and what was not
Depended on one single idea

何年何月　那時那刻
心中有城　城中有夢
夢醒何處　此身何存
見猶未見　知即不知
是點是線　若幻若真
虛實有無　定于一念

City Dream #9
城夢之九
Ink,Watercolour and Acrylic on Paper
157.5 x 96.5 cm, 2004

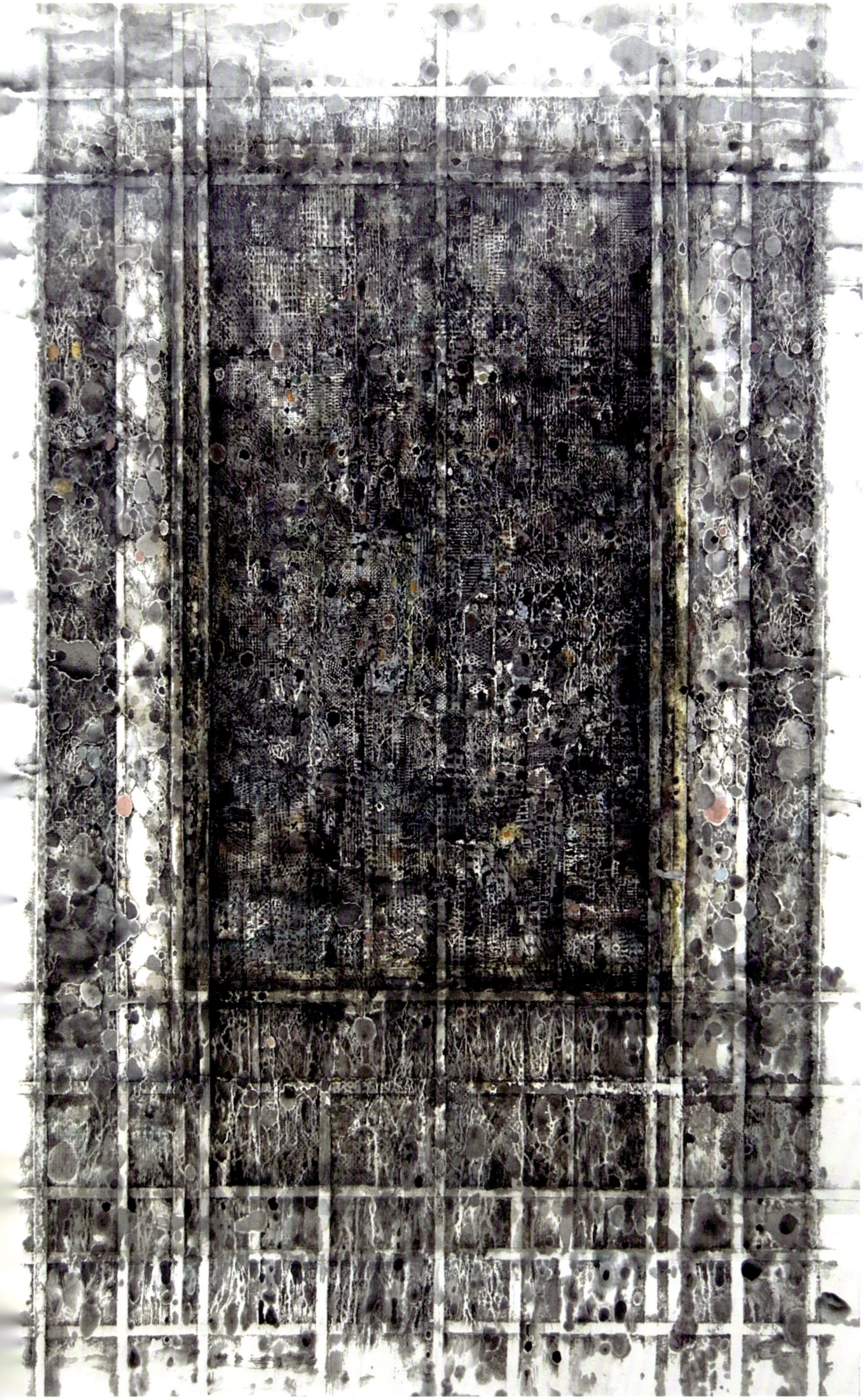

We are all trapped inside the matrix of the city. Here we eat, we move, we work, we sleep, and we dream.

城市是無所不在的巨型網絡。
我們生于斯，
居于斯，
食于斯，
工作于斯，
睡于斯，
夢于斯。

I lived on the mid-levels of the Hong Kong Island when this series of work was painted. Skyscrapers completely filled my vision. I saw one of Hong Kong\s tallest buildings grow up floor by floor right in front of my living room window. Natural scenery was completely blocked, and existed only in the dreams.

我居住于港島半山時寫成「城夢」系列，當時視野所及，盡是高樓大廈。我見到香港最高的一座摩天大廈，在客廳窗外，逐層增長。自然山水，早受隱蔽，只存在夢中。

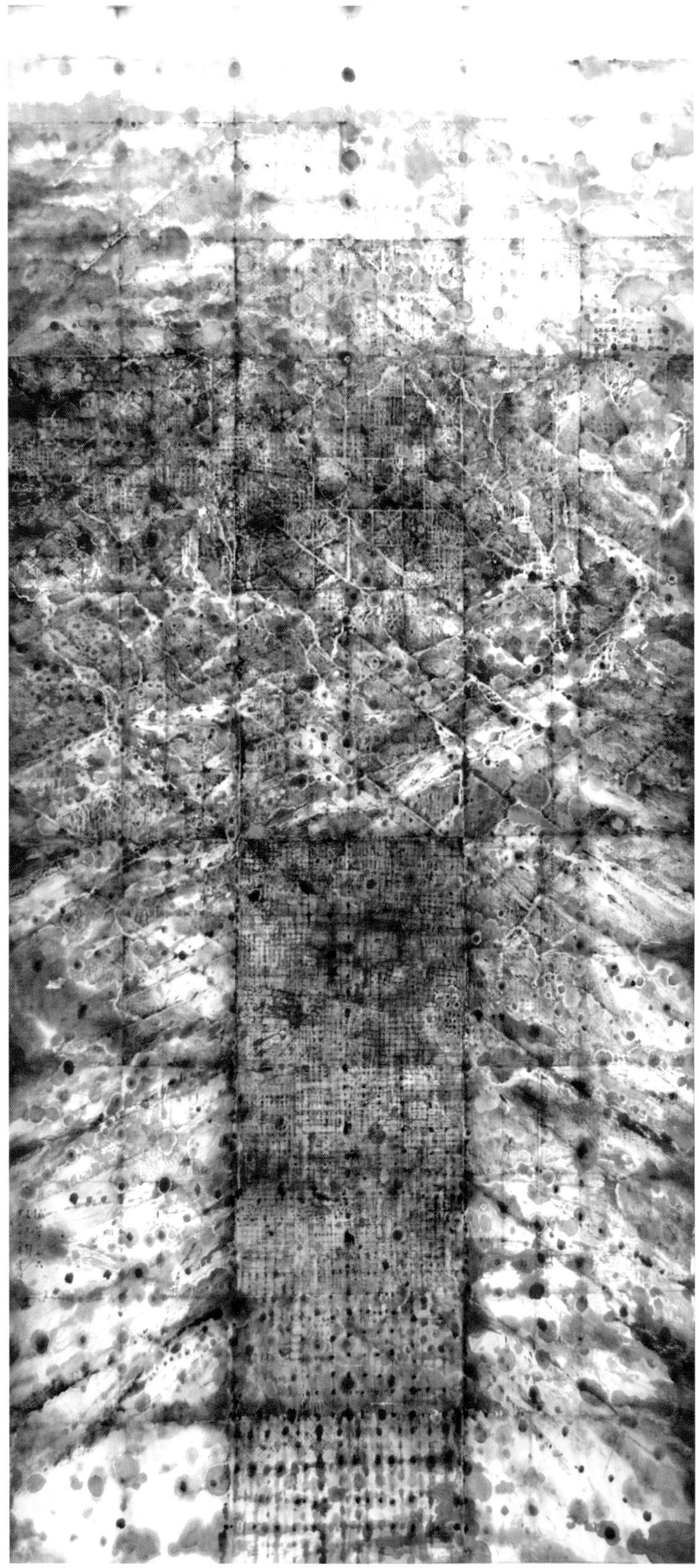

City Dream #6
城夢之六
Ink,Watercolour and Acrylic on Paper
217 x 99 cm, 2003

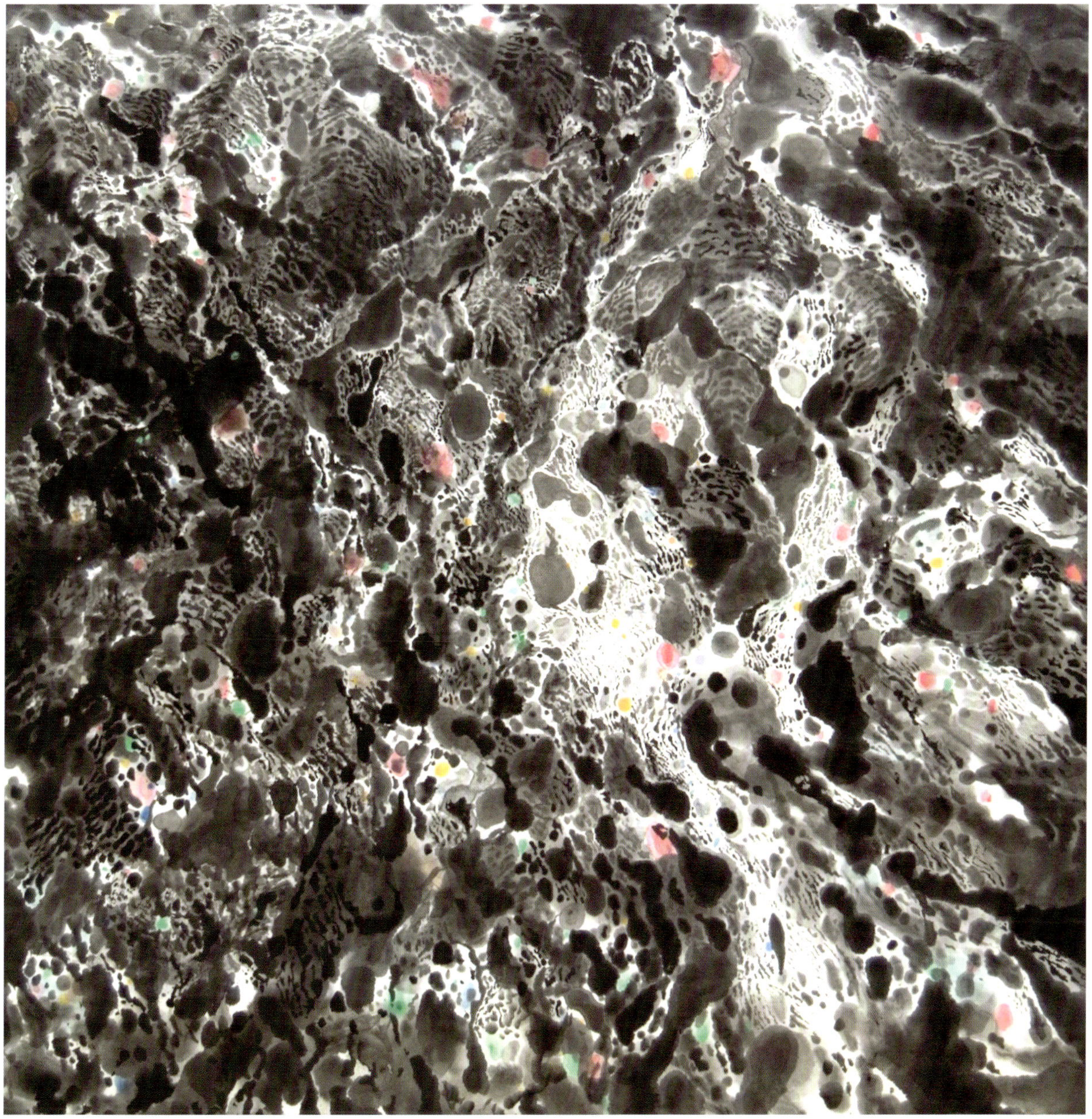

Water has no definite shape. Its inner nature is movement. It moves to show life. It spills on a flat surface, rushes through a gap, jumps with sharply sloping land, and fills a depression. It creates rhythm and tempo in a melodic progression.

水無定形，其性為動，
能動則活，活則流，
遇平則瀉，遇缺則衝，
遇陷則躍，遇凹則注，
以動靜緩急形成韻律節奏。

Flowing Water #4
流水之四
Ink,Watercolour and Acrylic on Paper
98 x 98 cm, 2007

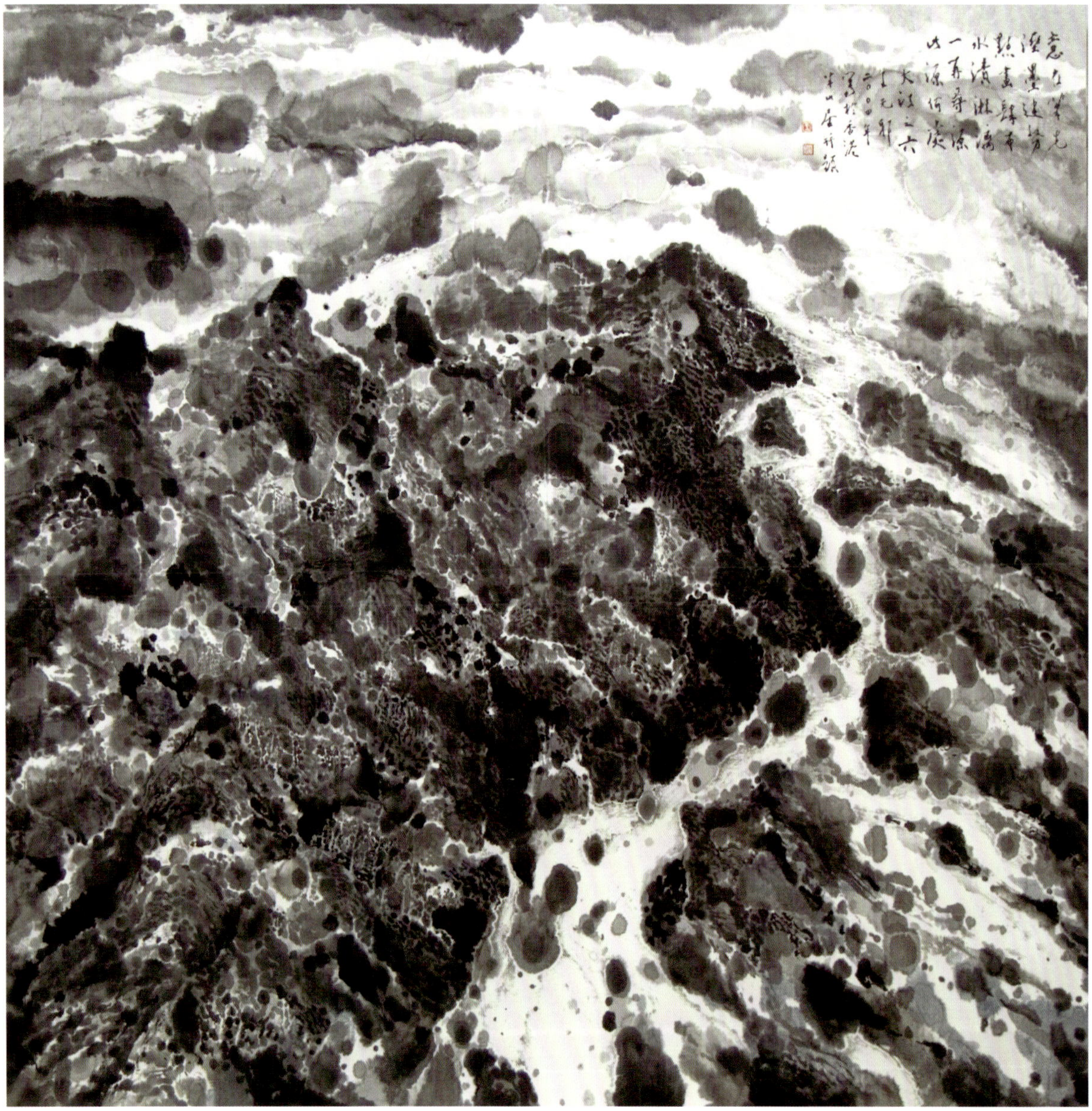

Idea precedes brush movement
Wet ink generates momentum
Dots and lines spread in space
Water penetrates and makes stains
Seeking the source again and again
Where can we discover the source?

意在筆先　溼墨建勢
點畫肆布　水漬淋漓
一再尋源　此源何處

The river has been a favorite theme. It represents fleeting time that can never be recovered. It also represents leaving the motherland and heading towards the unfathomable sea. Who does not sigh when days are gone forever?

移居海外又回流，我喜以江河作為主題。江水東流，湧向深不可測的大海，時間飛逝，往事如煙，能不感嘆？

Great River #6
大江之六
Ink,Watercolour and Acrylic on Paper
116 x 117 cm, 2004

Shitao said, "Ink can shape mountain and water, and brush can sweep them with powerful momentum." Recently, I attempted to use the brush loaded with diluted ink in an untrammelled manner to achieve the feeling of blowing wind and rolling clouds with masculine impact. My East-West journey now seems to swing more towards the East, to capture the rhythm and tempo of Nature in my own unique way.

石濤云
墨能栽培山川之形　筆能傾覆山川之勢
余近日學意筆縱橫
墨氣淋漓　寫成此作
此稍得風起雲湧之感　亦略現陽剛之美
東西雙向行中 今程偏東
希顯自然情懷　而見個人面目

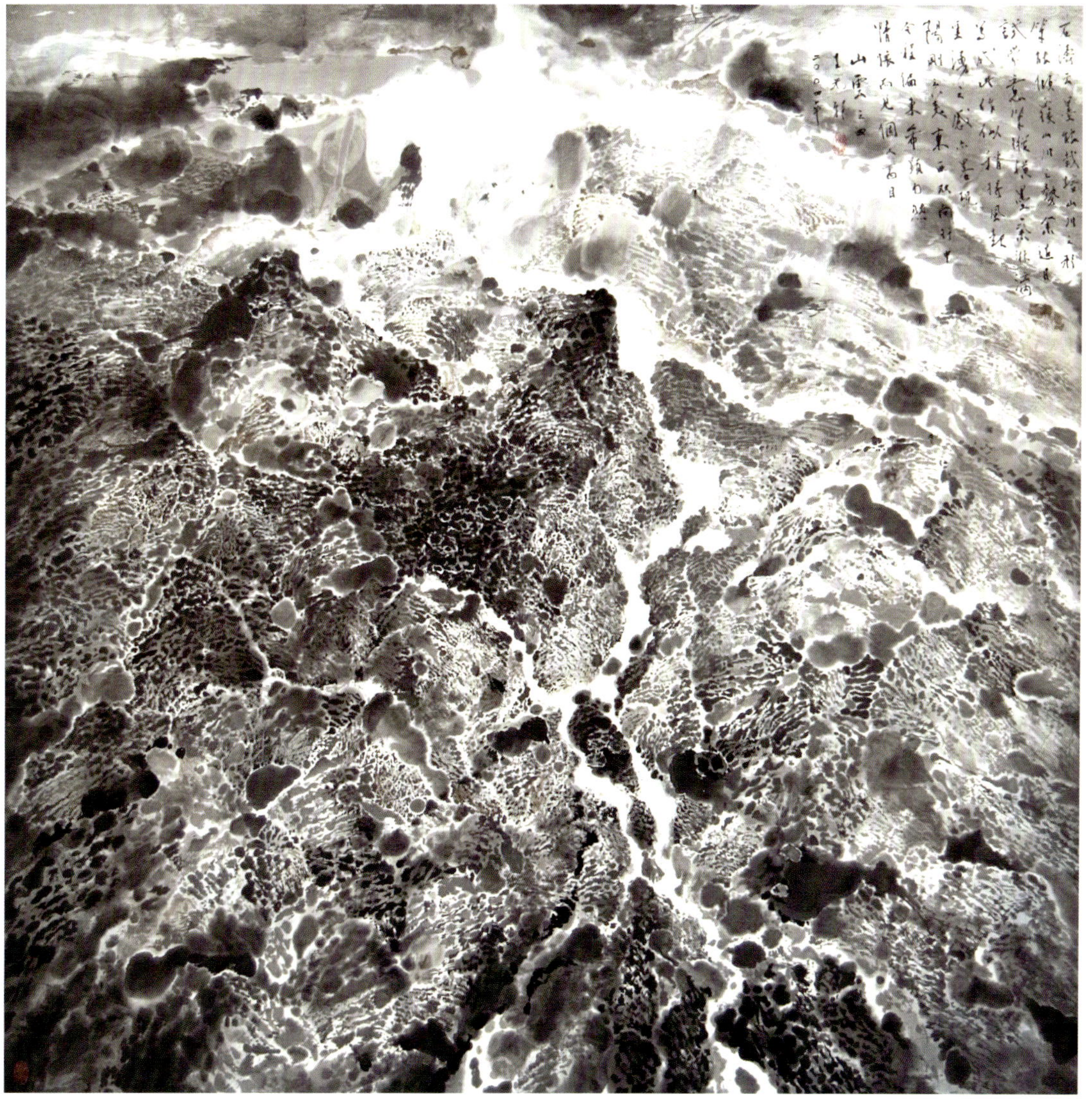

There is mountain. There is water. There should also be clouds to set the momentum, and to implement a complete spiritual circulation with perpetual movement.

有山。有水。更要有雲。然後有律動的生命，有旋轉不停的勢。

Mountain Clouds #4
山雲之四
Ink,Watercolour and Acrylic on Paper
97.5 x 95.5 cm, 2004

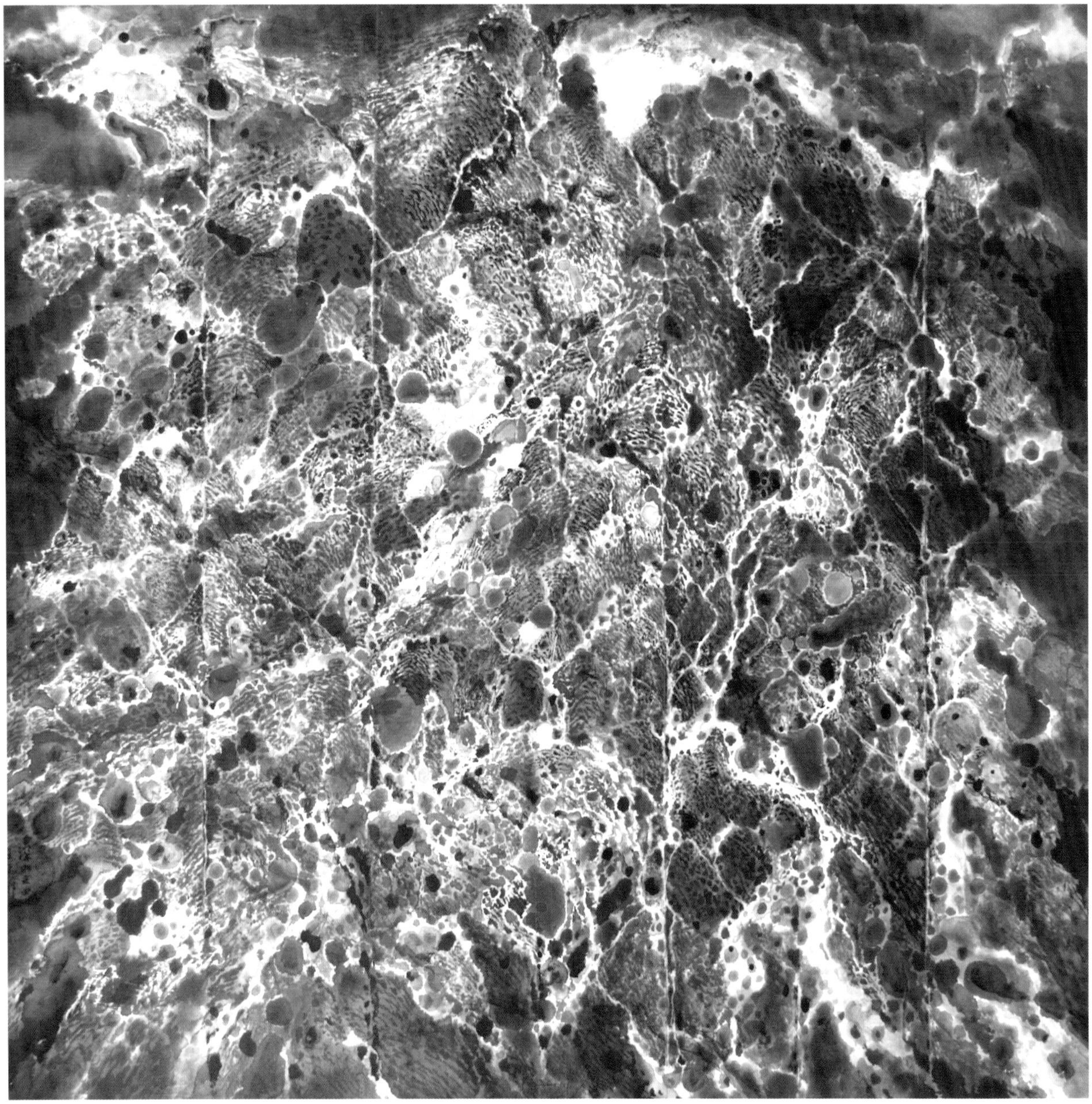

Wandering inside a mountain, one sees the mountain but does not really notice the mountain. Surrounded with trees and shrubs, finding streams and springs, treading the paths and climbing the slopes, one can fuse with Nature in the deep tranquillity.

漫步山中，見山未必見山，
高樹密林，曲澗飛泉，
危坡險徑，幽深中乃可忘我。

Deep In The Mountains #4
深山之四
Ink,Watercolour and Acrylic on Paper
68.5 x 68.5 cm, 2005

Clear sky buoys the land. Clouds fleet to suit the Autumn day (poem by Shen Zhou). Autumn in the South might show some bare trees and fallen leaves. It nevertheless provides us a clear and bright environment that seems more comfortable than the damp Spring or the hot Summer seasons.

天空欲浮地，雲盡最宜秋。
--沈周詩句
南國之秋，略見疏樹禿枝，
一片明淨，無春日之潮溼，
無夏日之炎熱，更使人展懷。

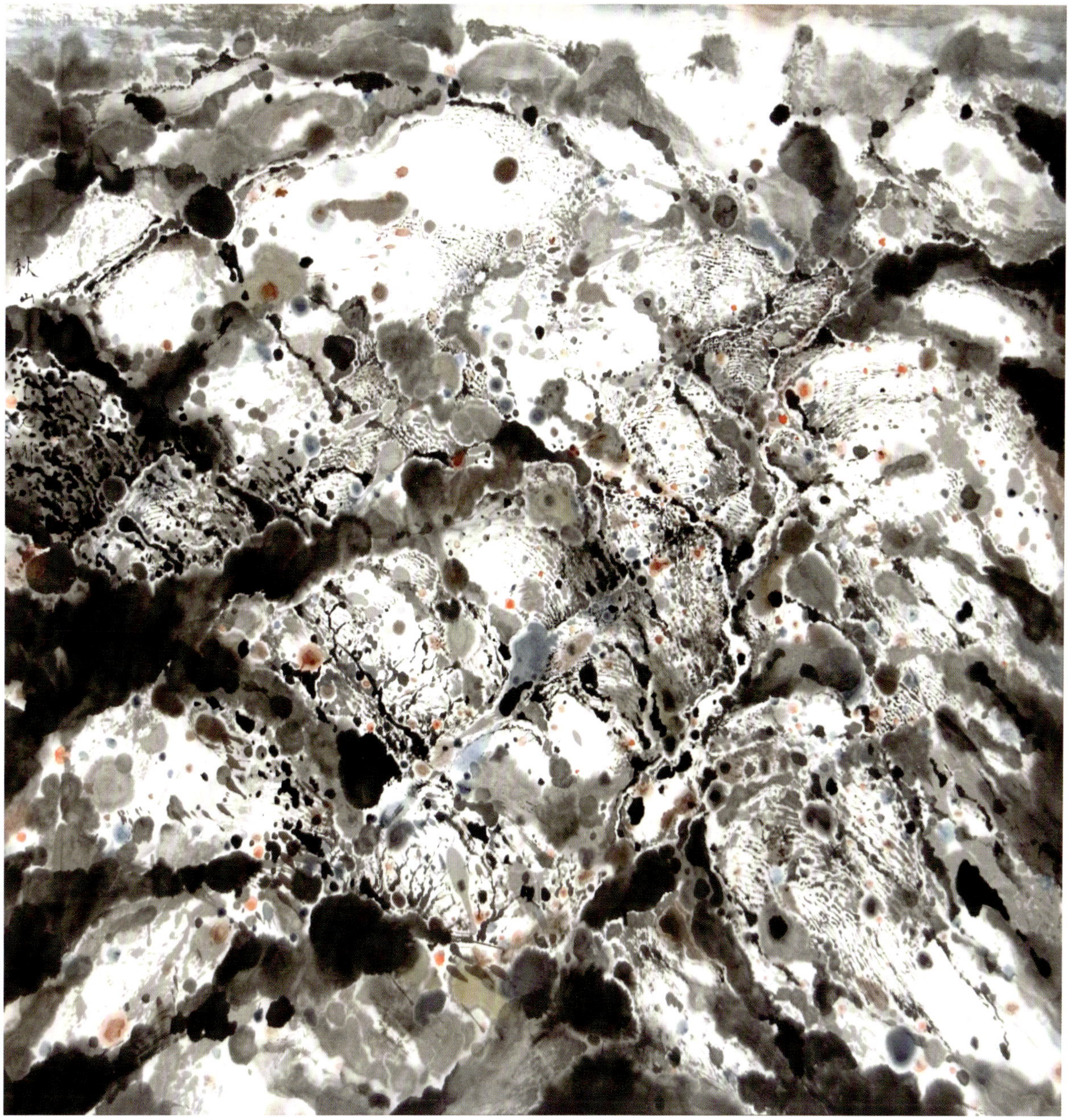

Autumn Mountain
秋山
Ink,Watercolour and Acrylic on Paper
66 x 66 cm, 2006

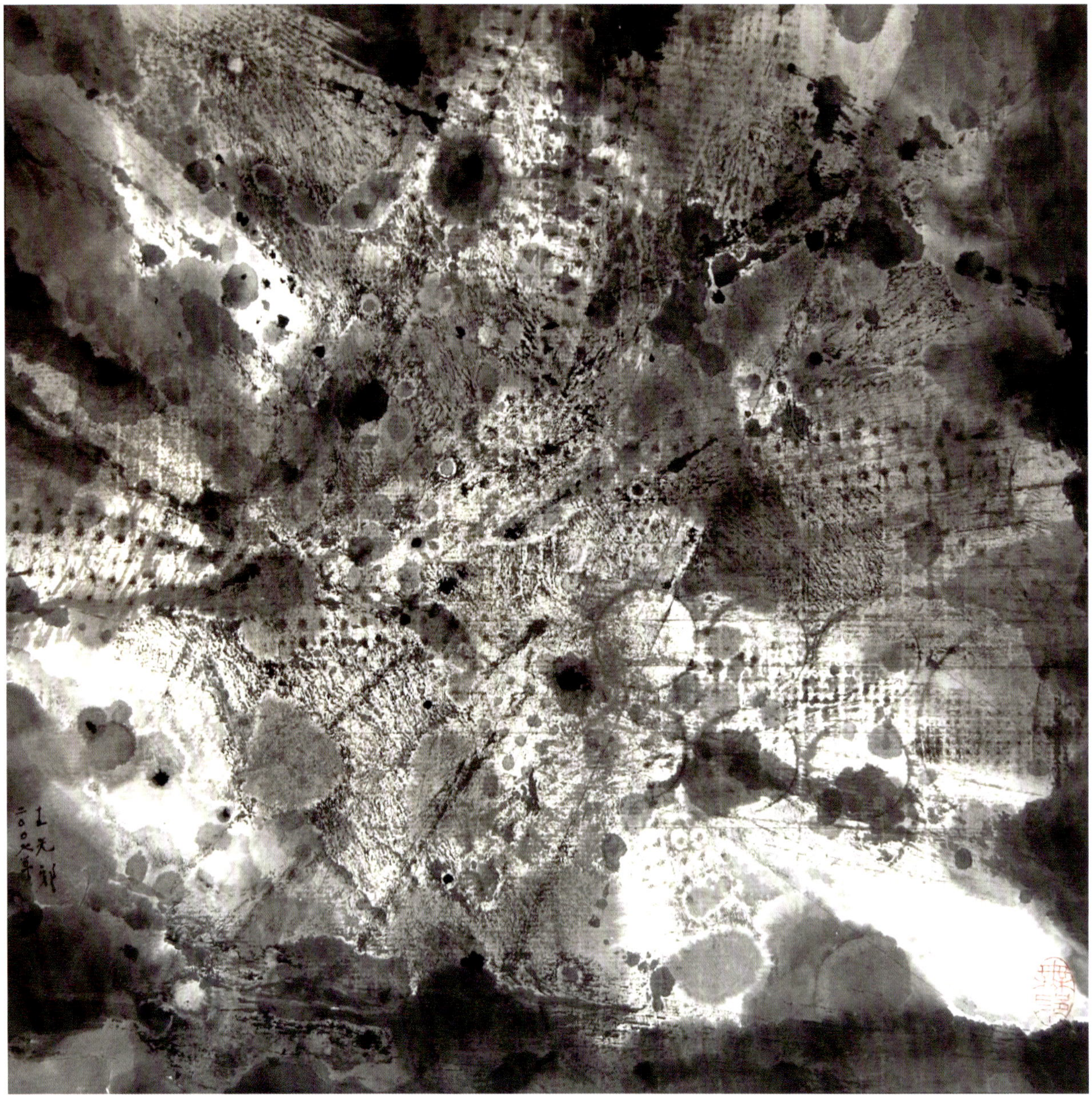

This is part of a series of experimental work partially created in front of students as demonstrations, merging free brushwork with geometric elements to express the feeling of urban living.

此作是實驗小品組畫中的一幀，先在課堂上于學生之前示範，後加潤飾完成，結合筆墨與幾何直線，表現城市人感情。

Dinghai Experiment #13
丁亥小品十三
Ink,Watercolour and Acrylic on Paper
32 x 32 cm, 2007

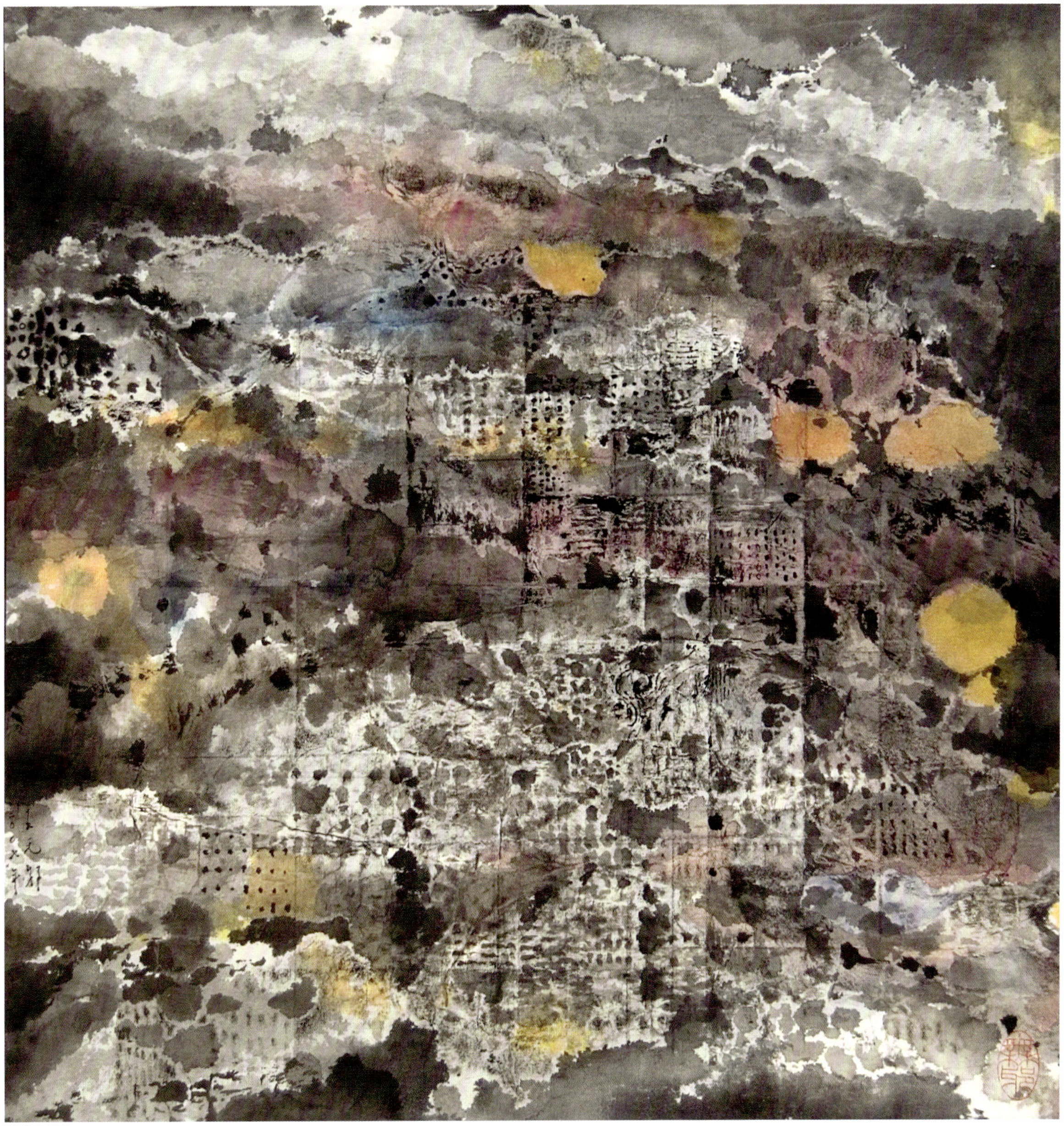

Here shows multi-storey buildings proliferate on the steep slopes of the Hong Kong Island.

此小品顯示港島依山而建的多層樓宇。

Dinghai Experiment #14
丁亥小品十四
Ink,Watercolour and Acrylic on Paper
32 x 32 cm, 2007

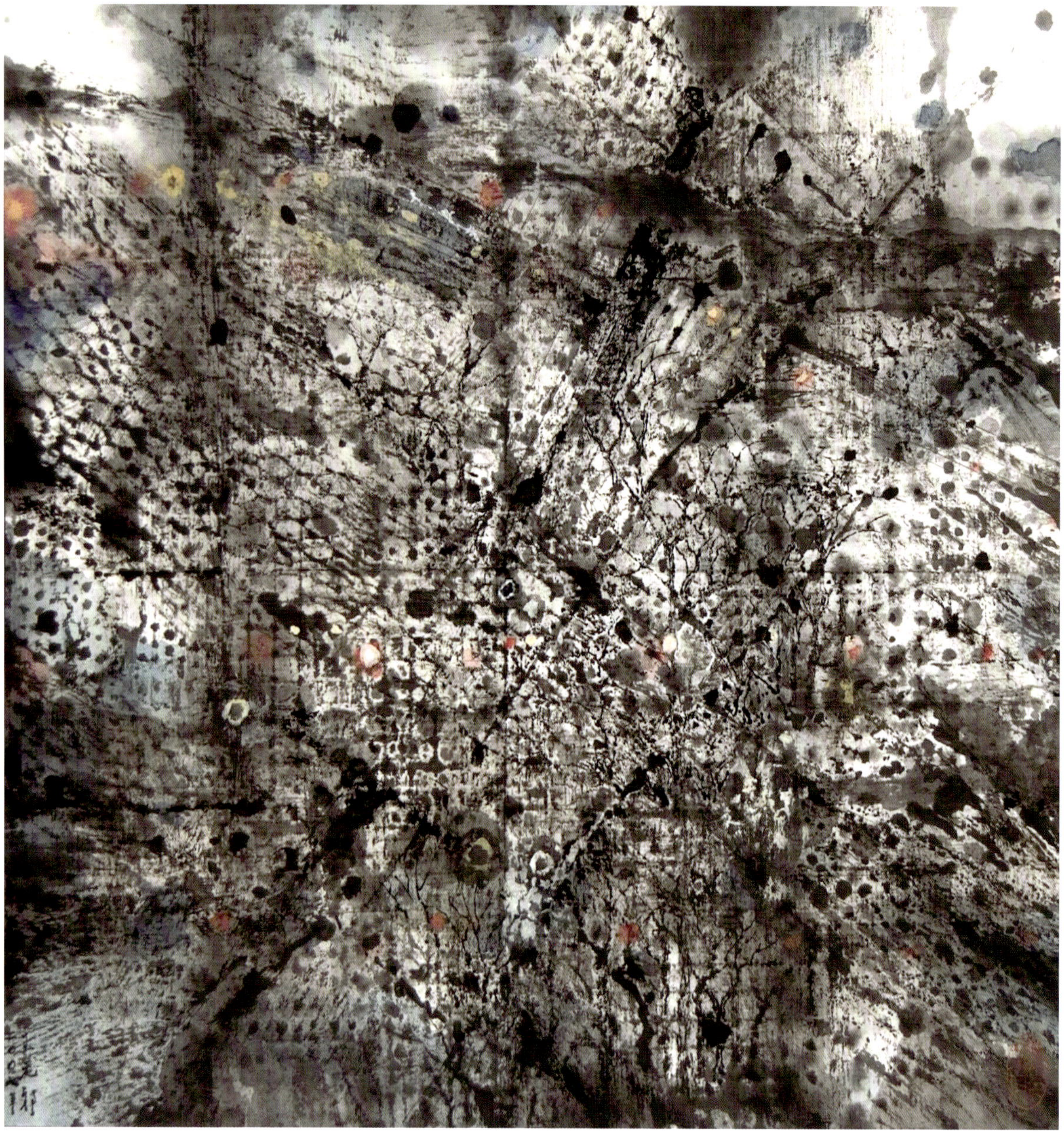

This experimental work expresses traffic jams and congestion in the city.

此小品表現城市的擠逼，及交通寸步難行之感。

Dinghai Experiment #15

丁亥小品十五

Ink,Watercolour and Acrylic on Paper

32 x 32 cm, 2007

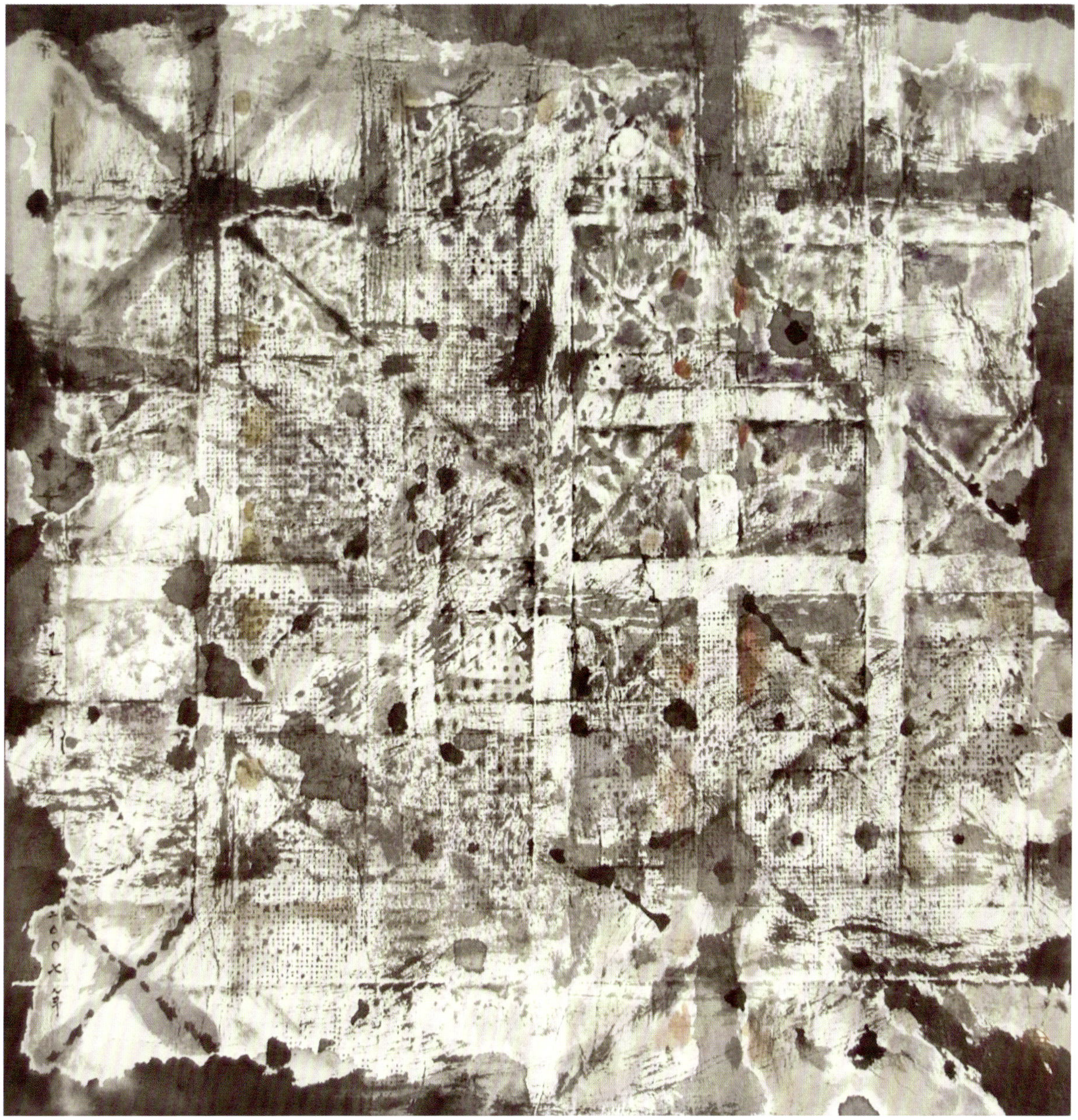

Destruction and construction are featured in this experimental work.

破壞與建設是此小品的主題。

Dinghai Experiment #16
丁亥小品十六
Ink,Watercolour and Acrylic on Paper
32 x 32 cm, 2007

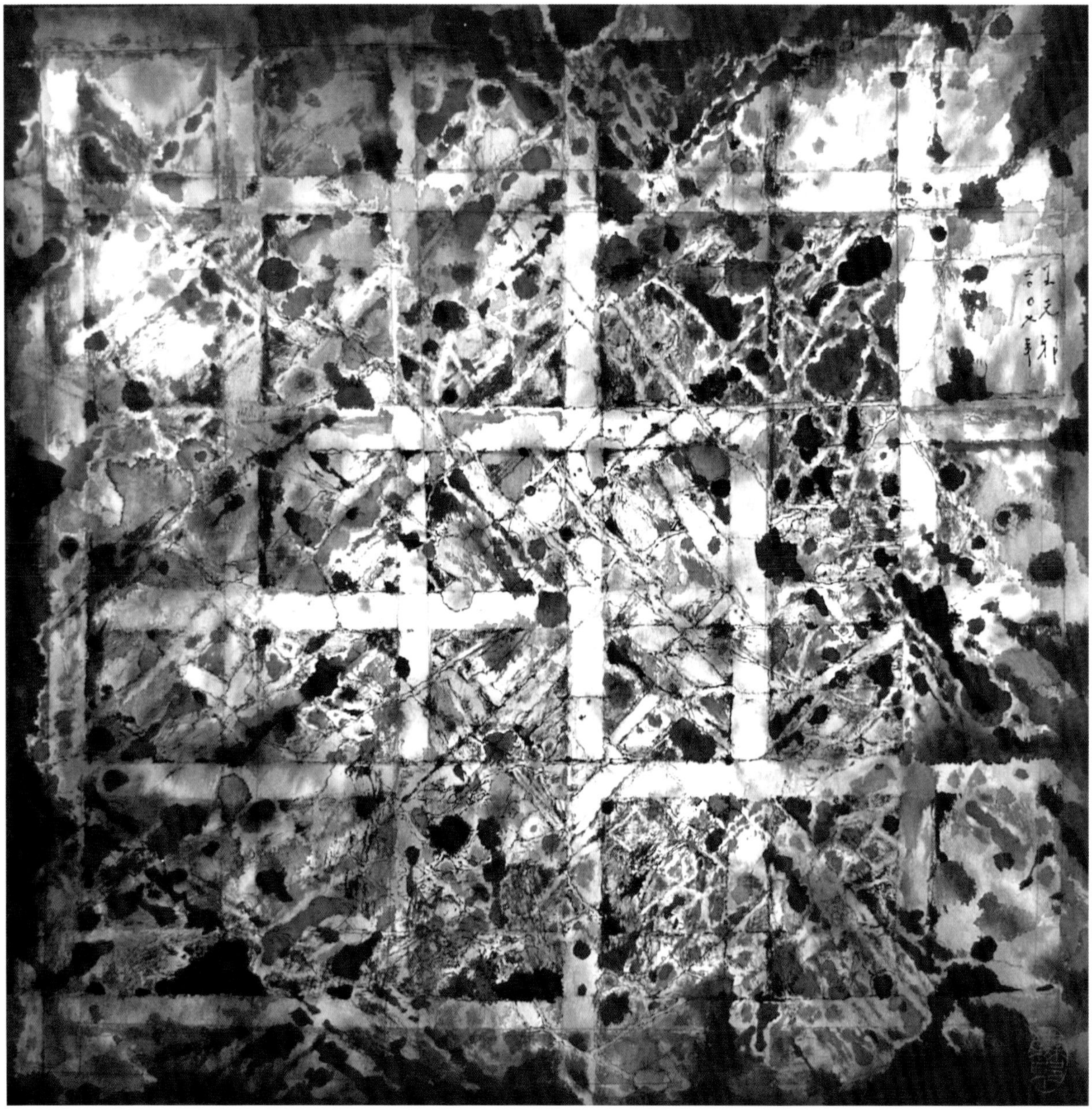

Partially built or partially deconstructed buildings are common sights in the city.
半建成或半拆毀的建築，是城中常見景象。

Dinghai Experiment #17
丁亥小品十七
Ink,Watercolour and Acrylic on Paper
32 x 32 cm, 2007

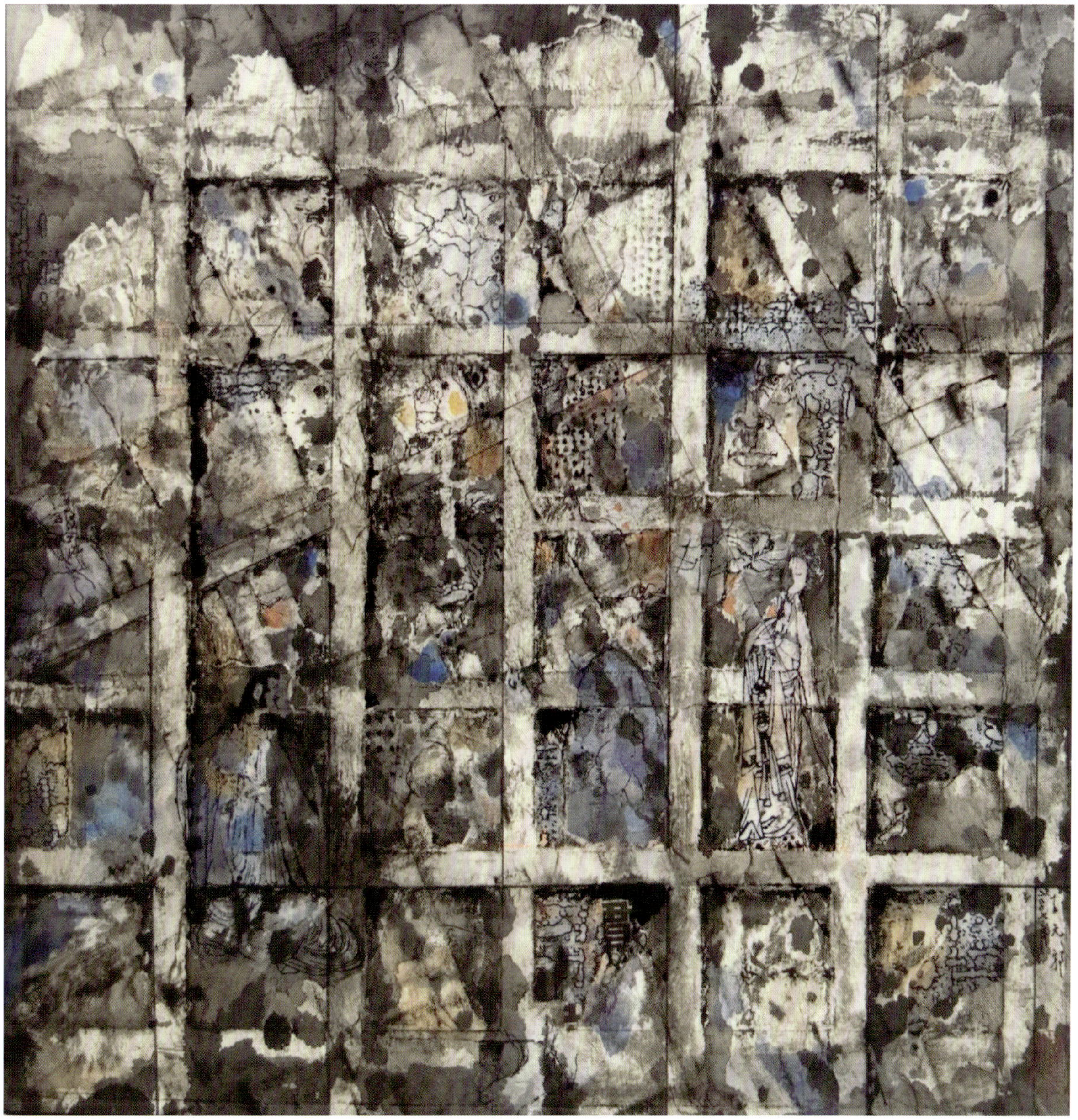

Fringed with high and low buildings, wide avenues and narrow streets devide this man-made environment. We all look into

人造環境中有道路縱橫，高廈林立，我們在其縫隙中尋找可以生活的空間。

Dinghai Experiment #18
丁亥小品十八
Ink,Watercolour and Acrylic on Paper
32 x 32 cm, 2007

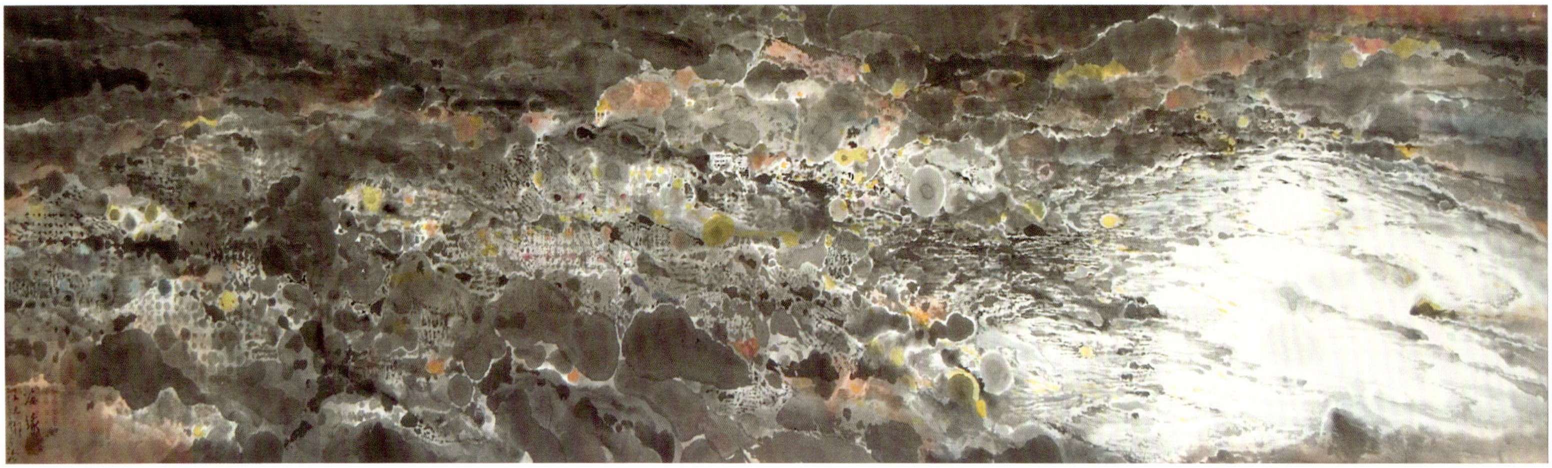

City dwellers yearn to get close to the sea or live by the sea, to listen to the sound of waves pounding the shore, to feel the coolness of the breeze, and to watch sundown.
城居者喜傍海而居，與海為鄰，得聆柏岸水聲，得受涼風吹拂，得見夕陽西下。

Edge Of Sea
海緣
Ink,Watercolour and Acrylic on Paper
33.5 x 135 cm, 2007

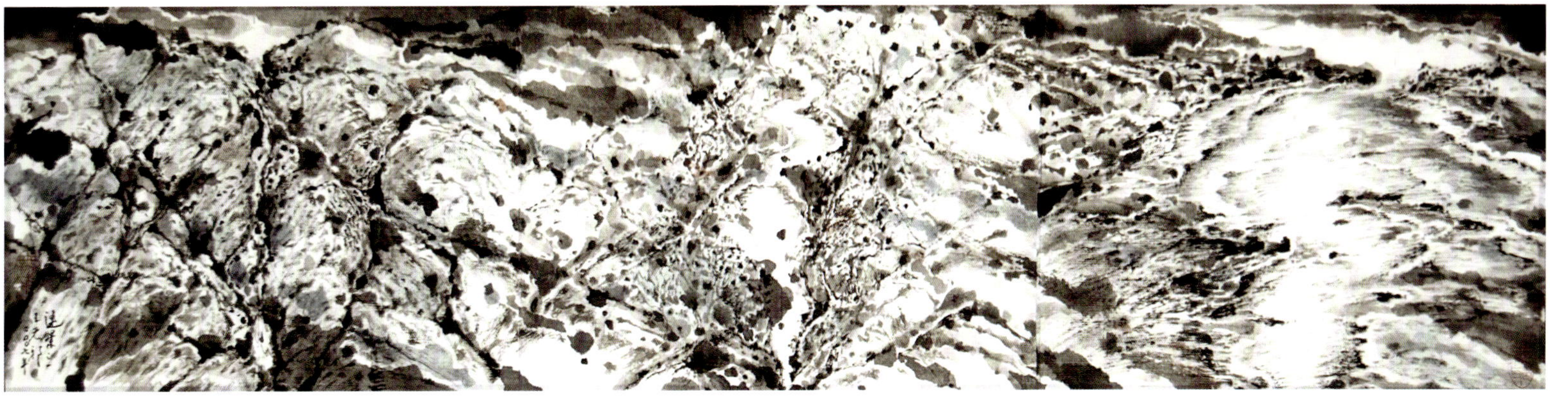

This painting, as part of a series' features small album leaves linked together. The join is sometimes noticeable revealing distinct separable spaces as added interest to the unified pictorial composition. Here from left to right water is presented as small waterfall, as lake, and as sea in a sequence.

此作是「連景」組畫之一，由小幅冊頁合併而成。相連的小幅經修飾後，接口不易見，但有時可見，三個獨立空間融合中又可分開，成為構圖特點。本畫由左至右，先有瀑布，繼而有湖，再有海，由小而大，產生漸變之趣。

Linked landscape #1
連景之一
Ink,Watercolour and Acrylic on Paper
17 x 70.5 cm, 2007

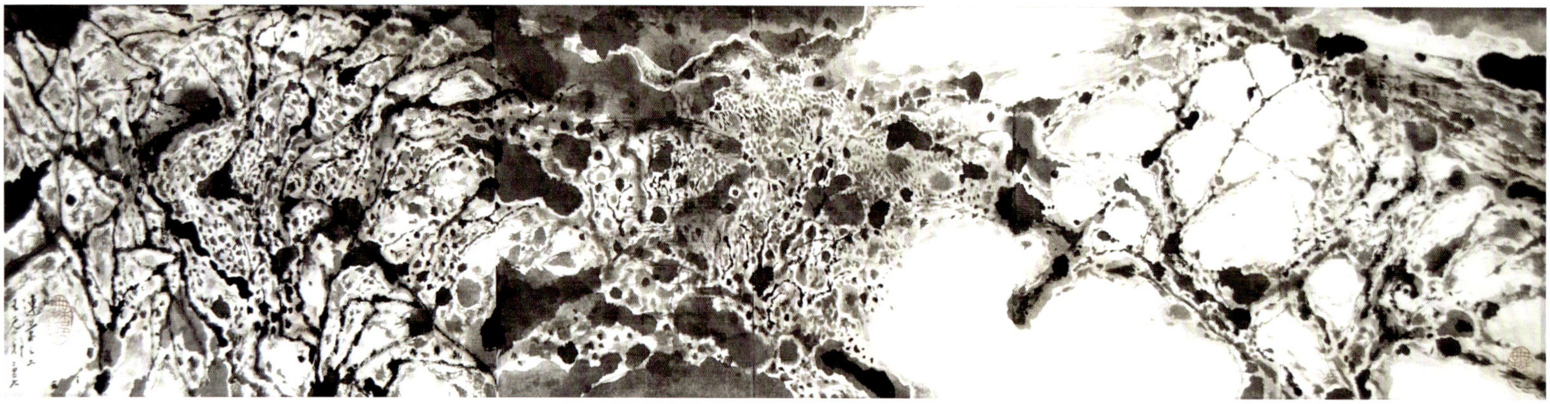

The three sections all show trees. The undulating branches and the dense and sparse leaves show rhythmical variations when all the sections are seamlessly fused.
三段連景，都是樹的主題，疏密間隔，造成節奏。

Linked landscape #2
連景之二
Ink,Watercolour and Acrylic on Paper
17 x 70.5 cm, 2007

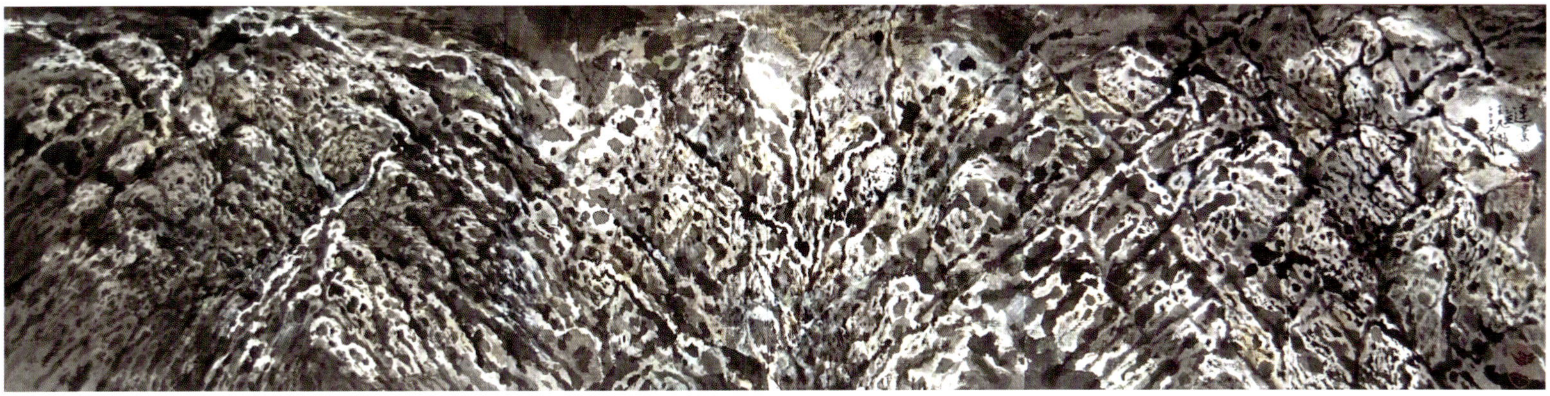

Here three land masses are linked into one single composition. Each land mass contains a dented area where a stream emerges. The streams run in different directions to form the composition.

三段都是山體，有凹陷部分，呈現溪瀑，而方向各異，構成完整合一的畫面。

Linked landscape #3
連景之三
Ink,Watercolour and Acrylic on Paper
16.5 x 70 cm, 2007

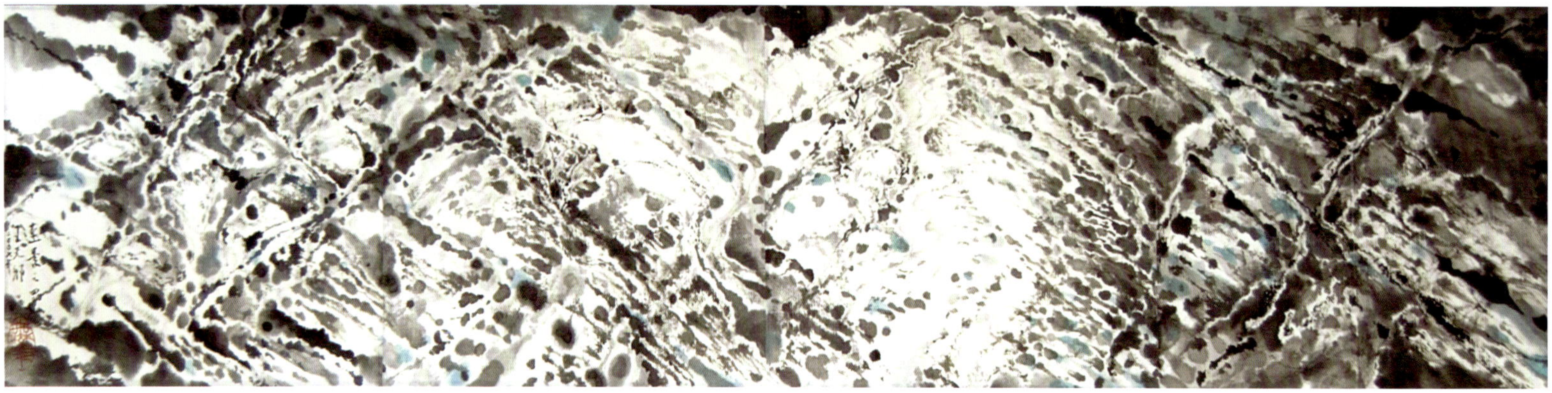

The theme in this work is water which appears as moving rhythms and light patterns in a unified expression.

此畫主題是水，三段表現不同流動的紋，並顯示旋律與光之變化。

Linked landscape #4

連景之四

Ink,Watercolour and Acrylic on Paper

15.5 x 70.5 cm, 2007

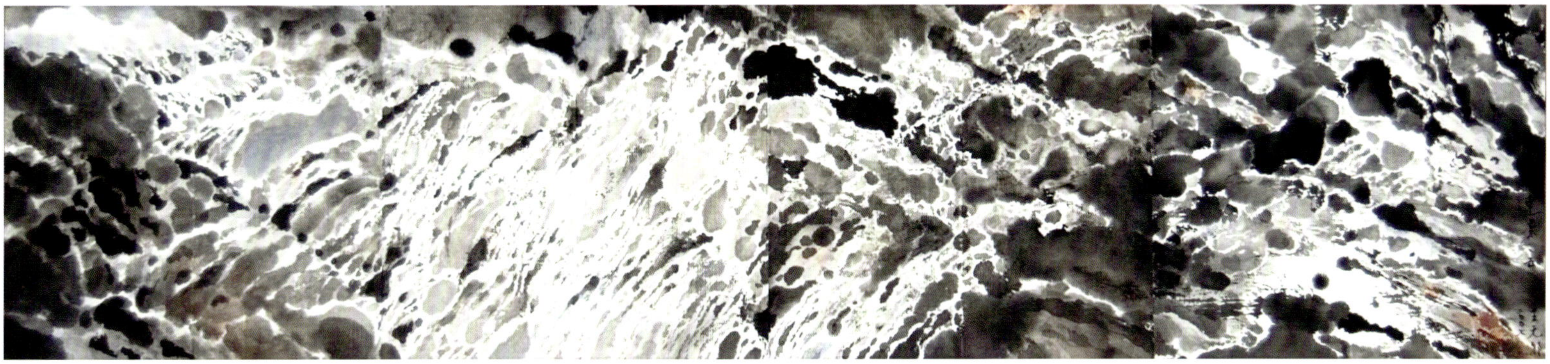

Here water is shown in different forms. In the left section, it is represented as waves. In the central section, it is represented as a waterfall. In the right section, it spreads on the marsh land.

不同形態的水在此組合。左段的水是波濤洶湧，中段有瀑布飛瀉，右段為泥濘沼澤。

Linked landscape #5
連景之五
Ink,Watercolour and Acrylic on Paper
15.5 x 70 cm, 2007

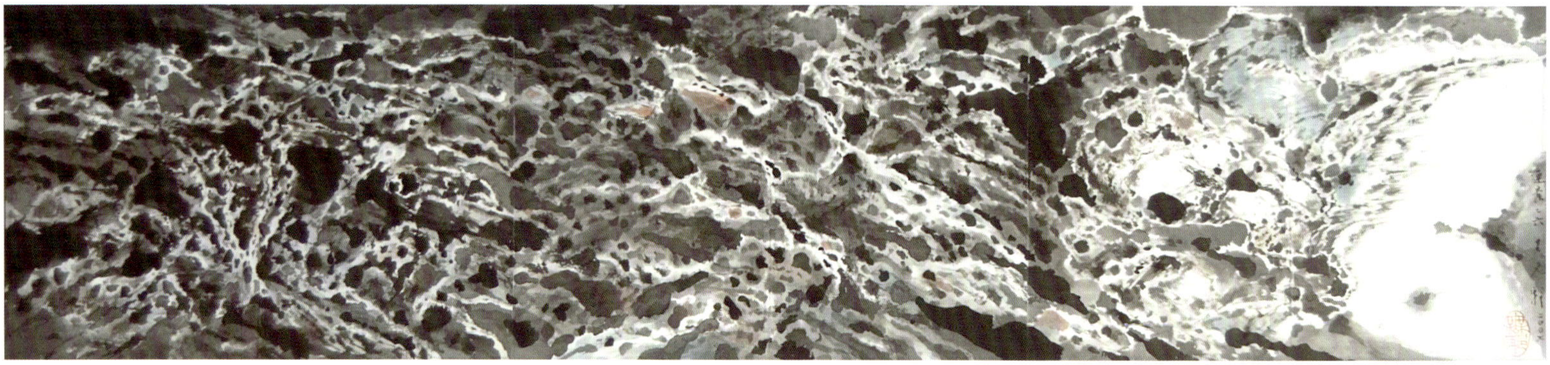

A land mass stretches from left to right. At extreme right, a river runs quietly. Trees and vegetation are emphasized in the left section. The land mass slopes gradually in the central section and forms a river bank in the right section.

畫中表現左段為高起的陸地，有樹有草或其他植物。中段陸地逐漸傾斜。右段出現河流。

Linked landscape #6
連景之六
Ink,Watercolour and Acrylic on Paper
16.5 x 70 cm, 2007

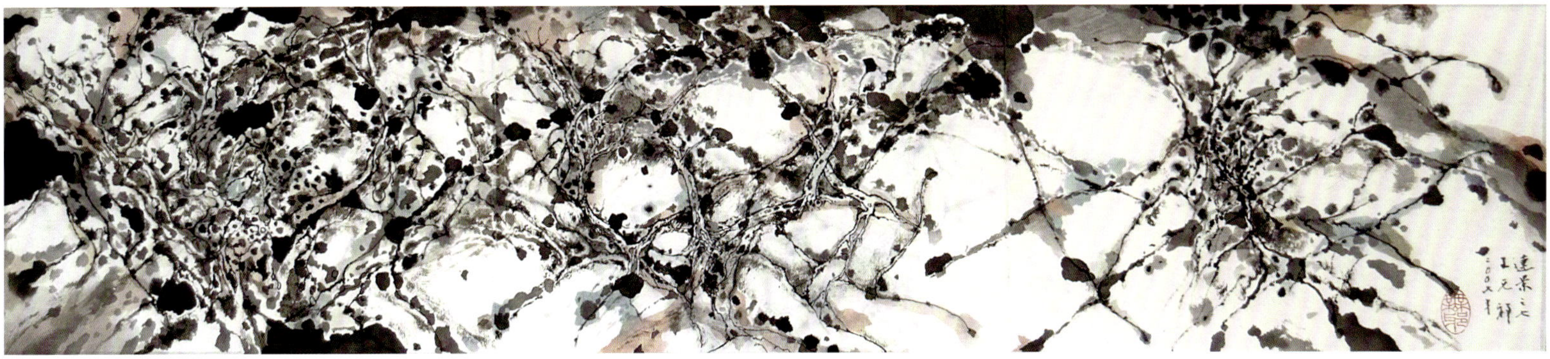

Similar to Link Landscape #2, this painting also features tree forms. Tree trunks and branches are shown in a curvilinear movement.
像「連景之二」，本畫亦表現樹，而特別強調樹幹與枝條之扭動姿態。

Linked landscape #7
連景之七
Ink,Watercolour and Acrylic on Paper
16 x 70 cm, 2007

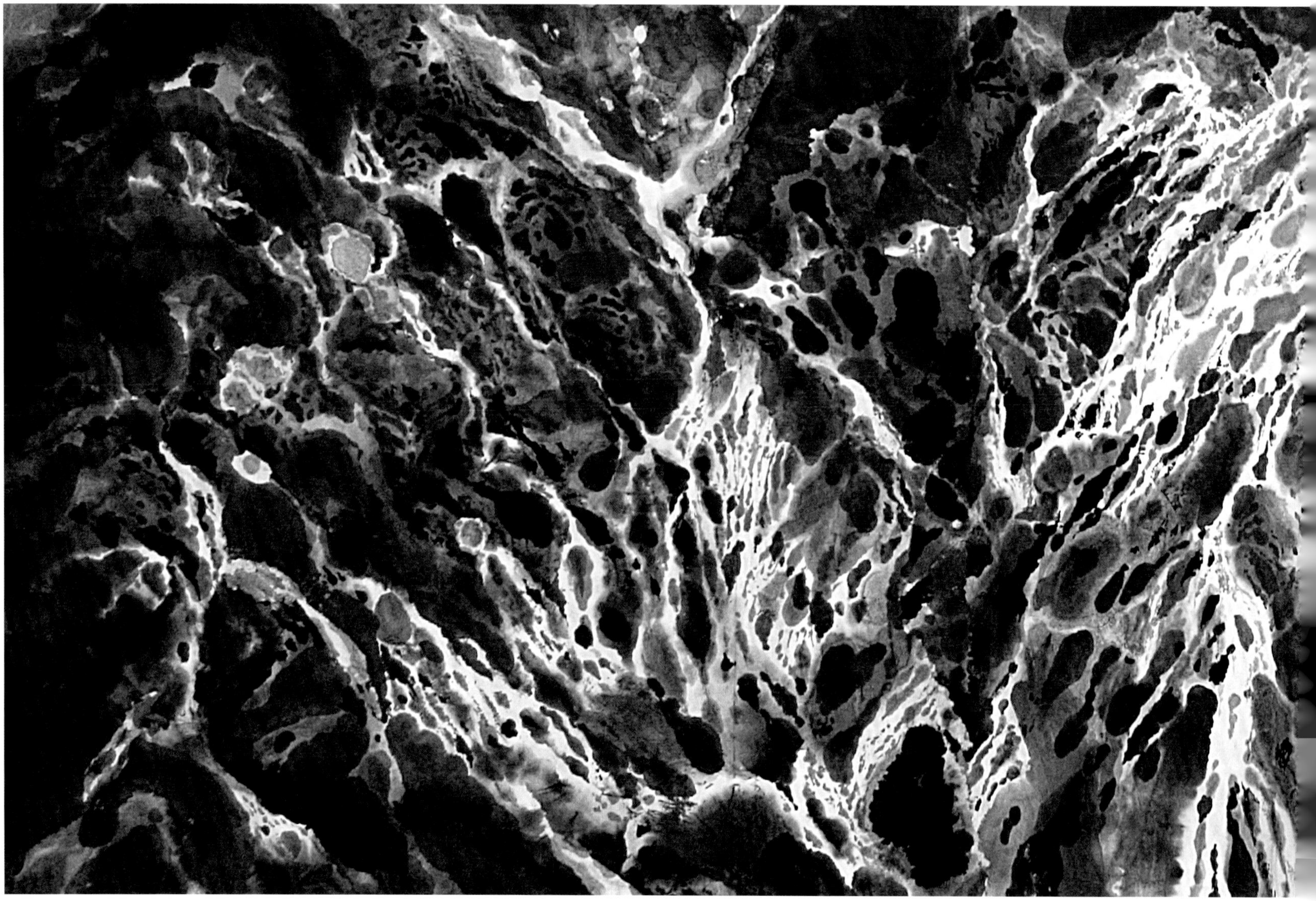

Running Water Forever #2
水長流之二
Ink,Watercolour and Acrylic on Paper
46 x 143.5 cm, 2007

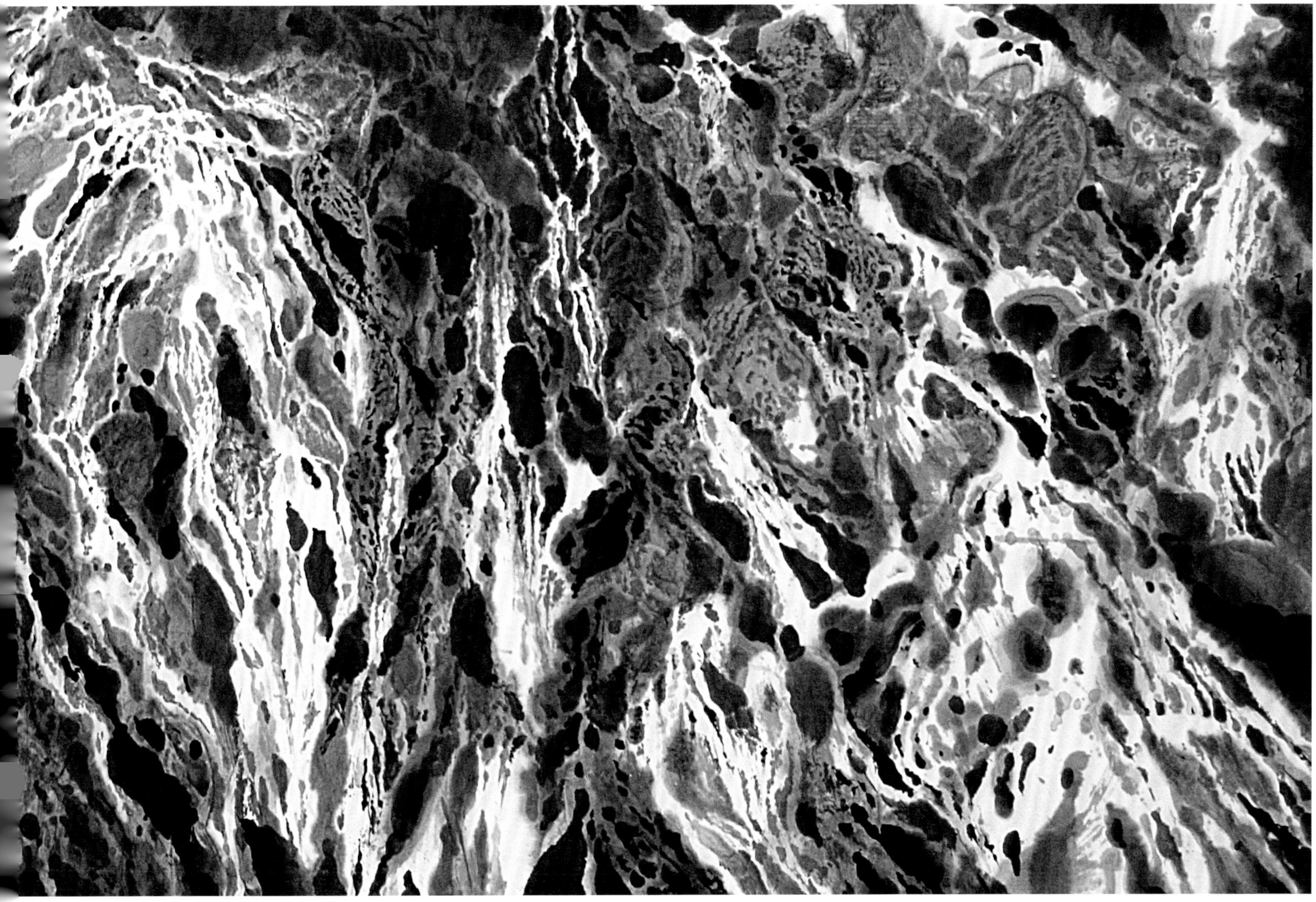

Rushing water draping the rocks in a waterfall is here shown at close-up. The central section makes the focal point.
此作以瀑布為主體，近觀岩石上流水衝瀉，具萬鈞之勢。中段為焦點所在。

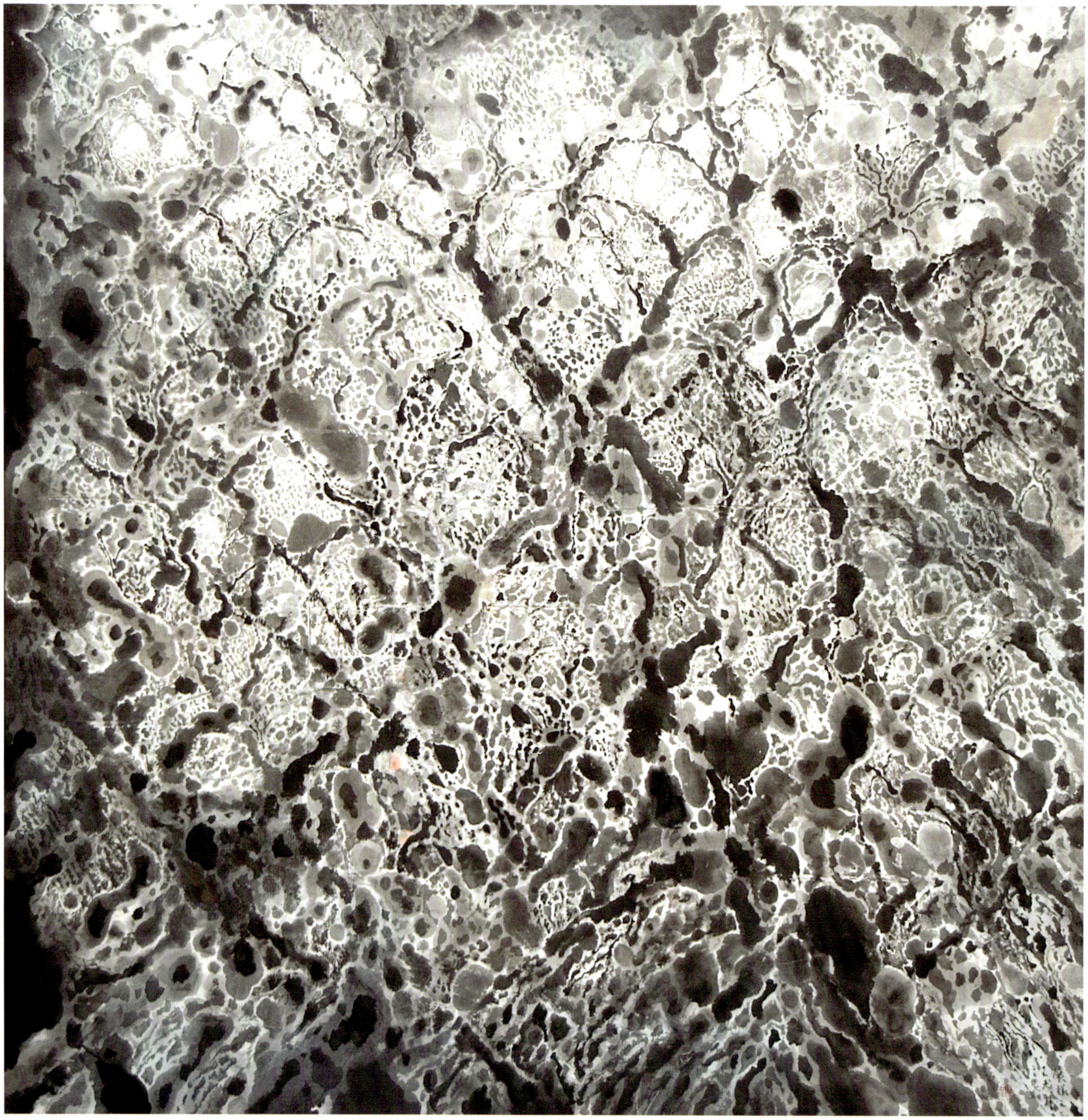

Trees stretch their trunks, branches and foliage to meet the sky. The painting, however, specifically emphasizes spreading of roots on the ground to symbolize craving to find settlement in a place.

樹以其幹與枝葉伸入天際，又以其根抓緊地面，展向泥土深處，代表遊子回歸心境。

Spreading The Roots #3
展根之三
Ink,Watercolour and Acrylic on Paper
80 x 81 cm, 2007

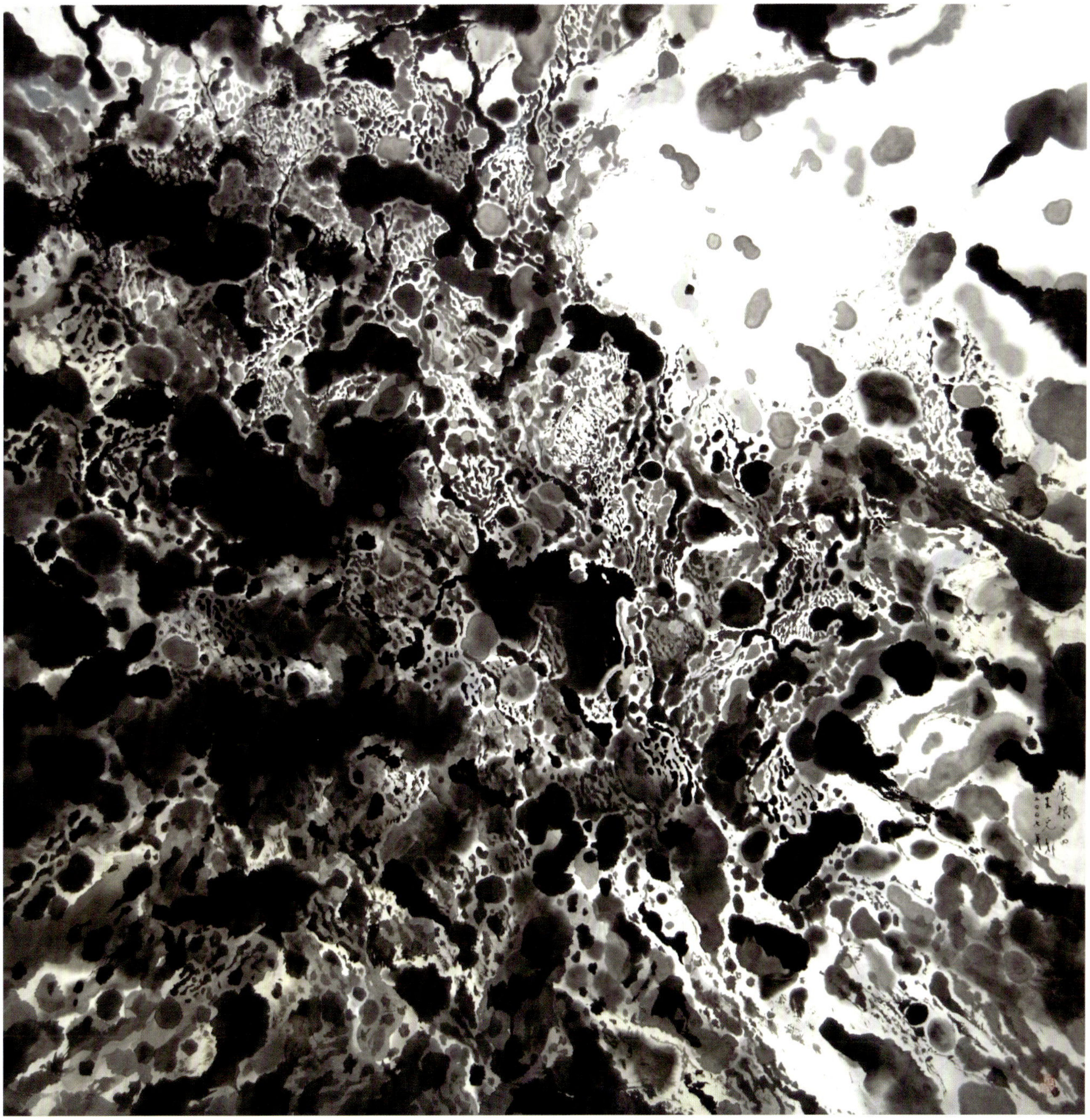

As the trees extend their roots on the soil, branches also stretch high to greet the bright day.

樹向地面展根，同時以枝條迎接晴朗的白晝。

Spreading The Roots #4

展根之四

Ink,Watercolour and Acrylic on Paper

87.5 x 87.5 cm, 2007

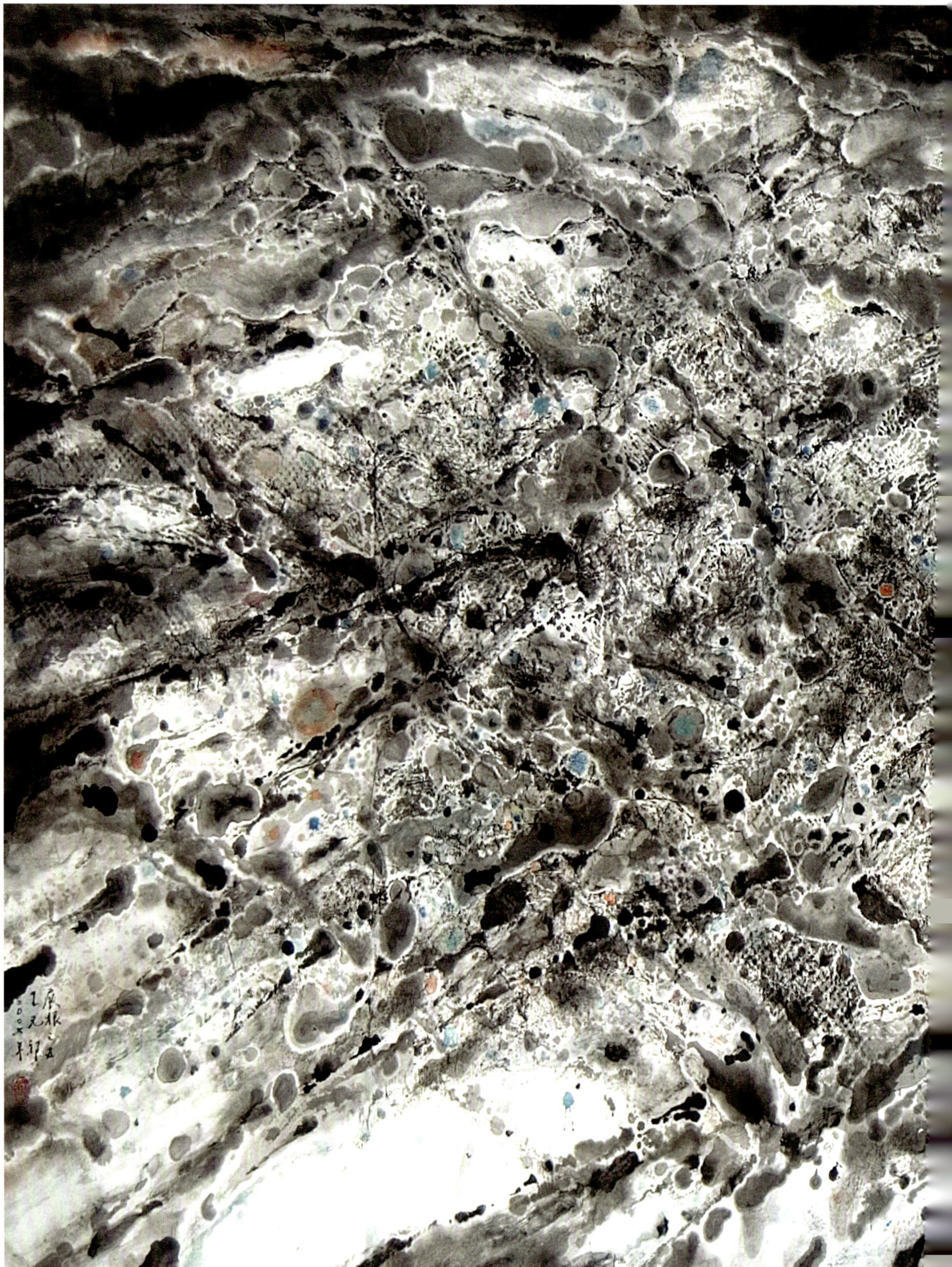

Spreading The Roots #5
展根之五
Ink,Watercolour and Acrylic on Paper
95 x 177 cm, 2007

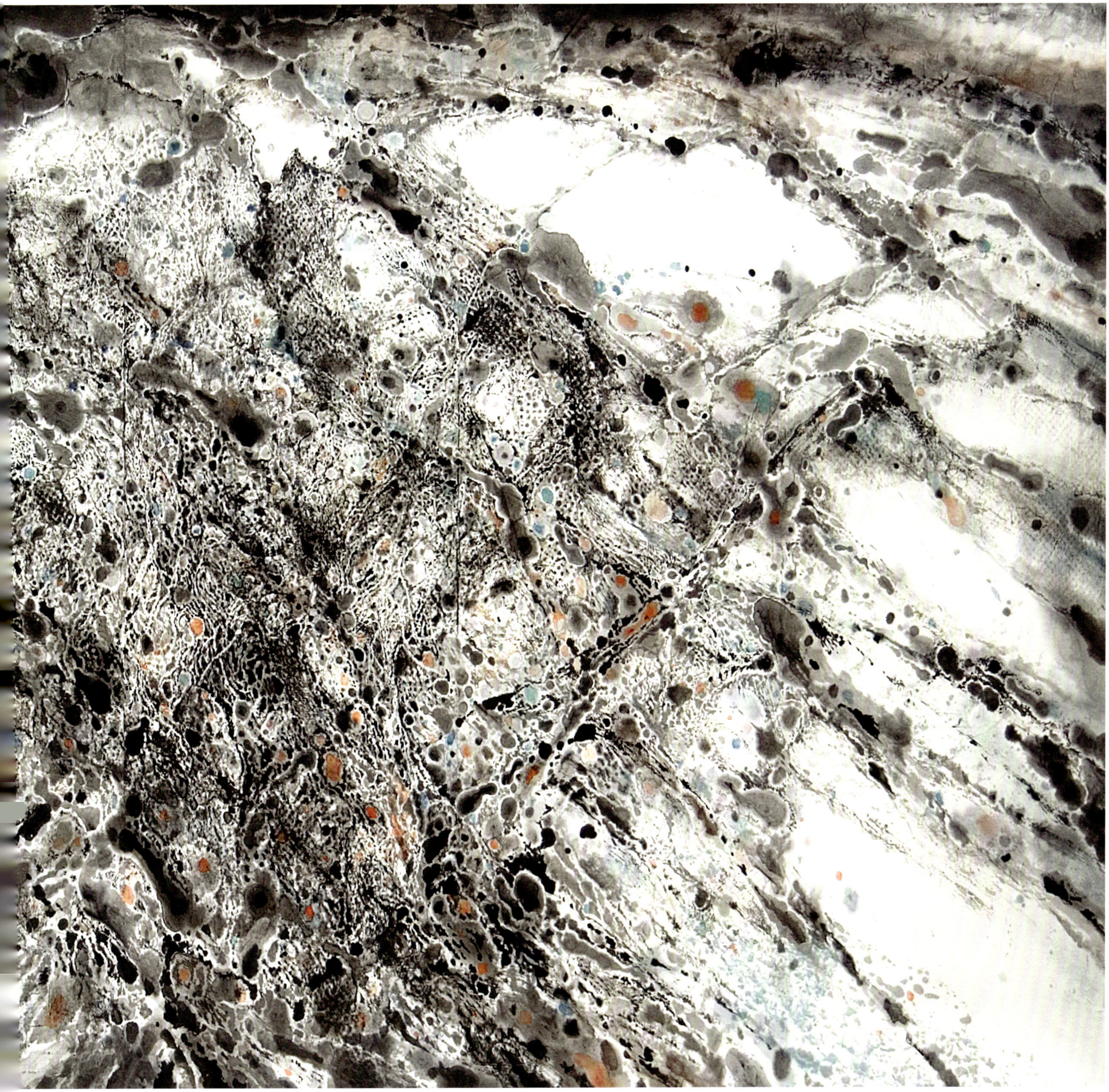

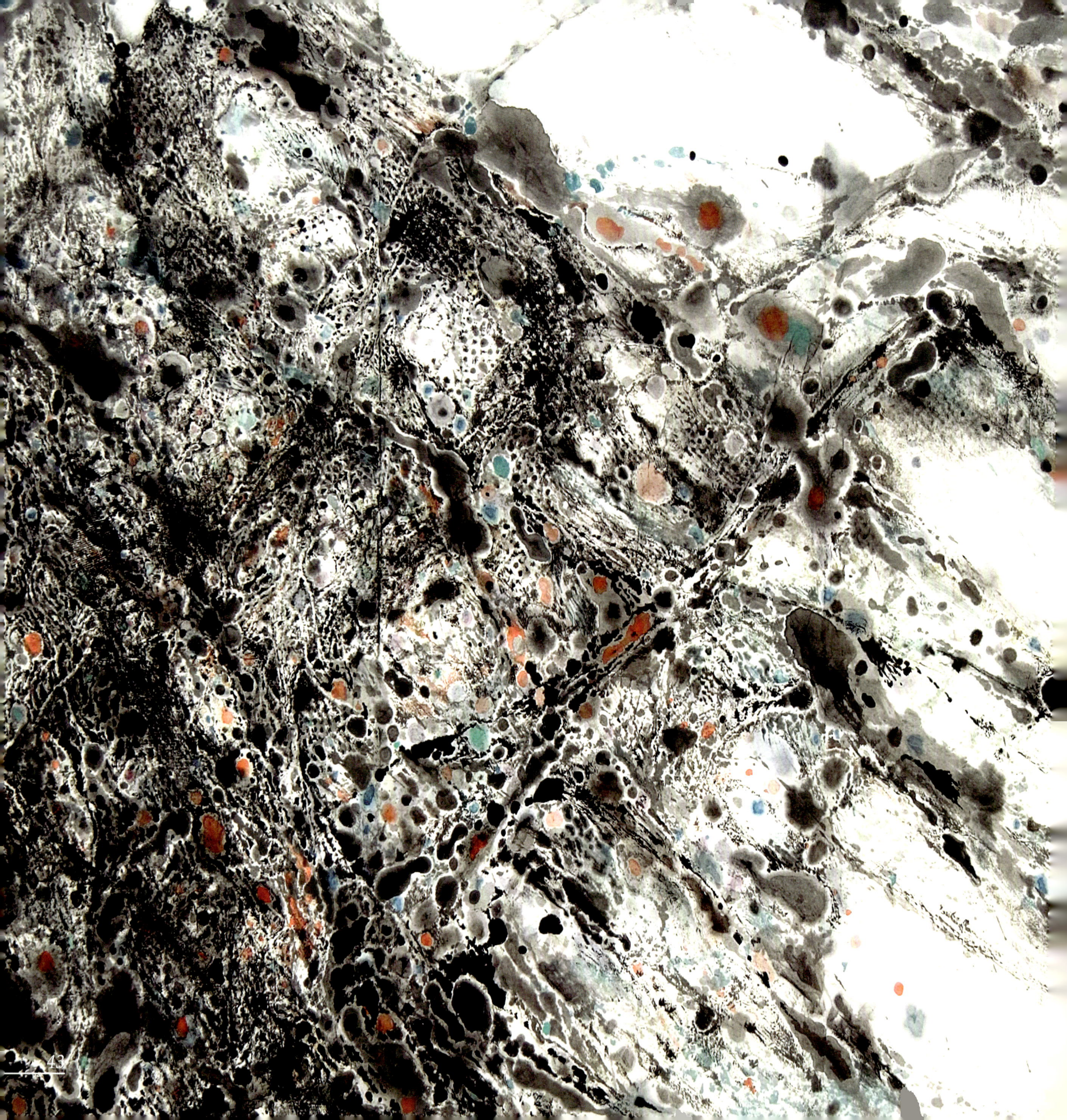

Spreads its roots, a magnificent tree further spreads its foliage to shade generations to come.
大樹展根，更廣散其葉，屹立于永恒中，蔭庇未來世代。

Partial detail of the right, Spreading The Roots#5
展根之五局部細節(右上)

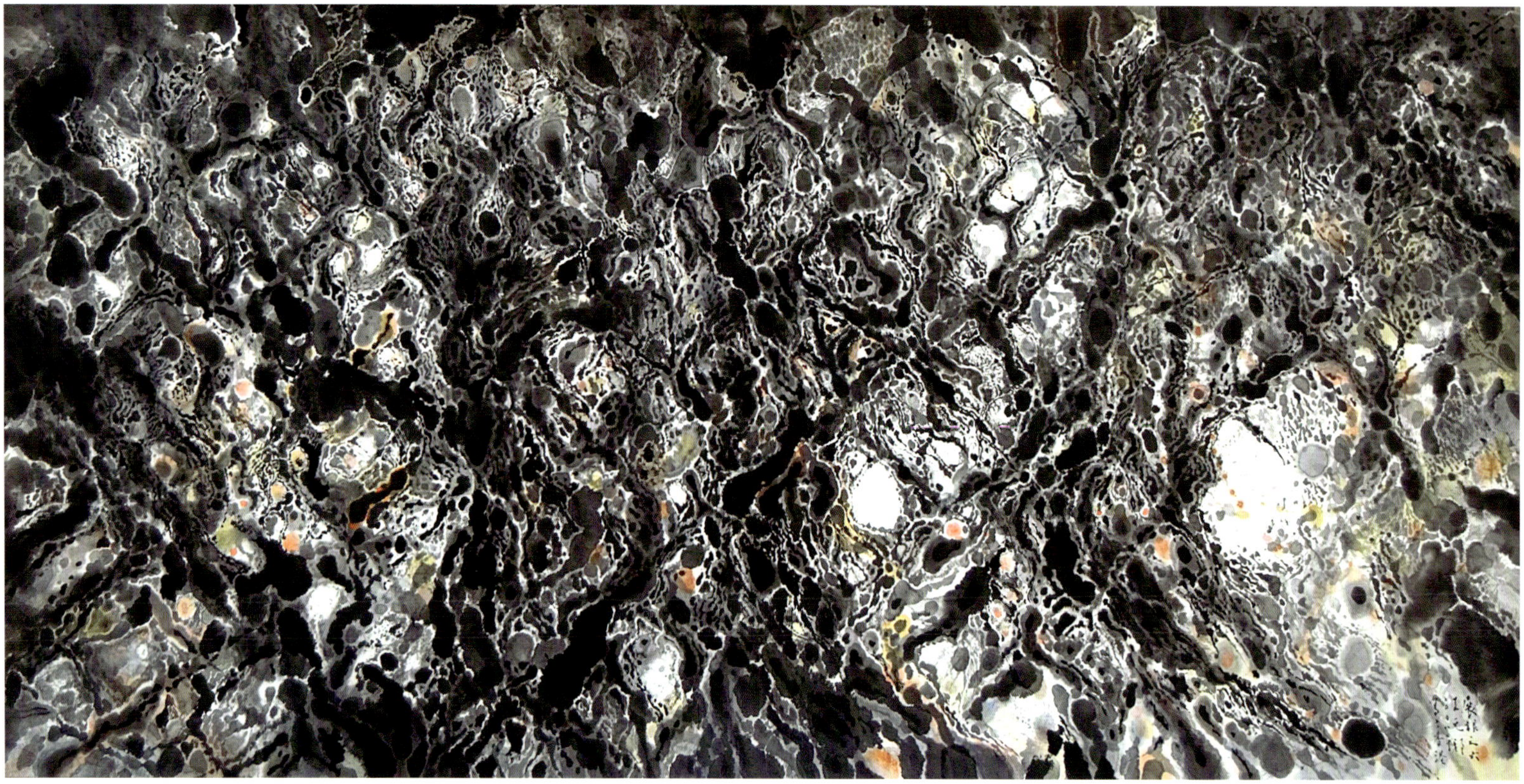

Trees gather to form forest, with trunks and branches entwined and roots sprawling in a closely knit pattern. Layered space reveals immense depth where vitality of life is concealed.

多樹叢生，則成密林，枝幹疊織，根莖交盤，幽深無盡，生機內蘊。

Spreading The Roots #6
展根之六
Ink,Watercolour and Acrylic on Paper
68.5 x 138.5 cm, 2008

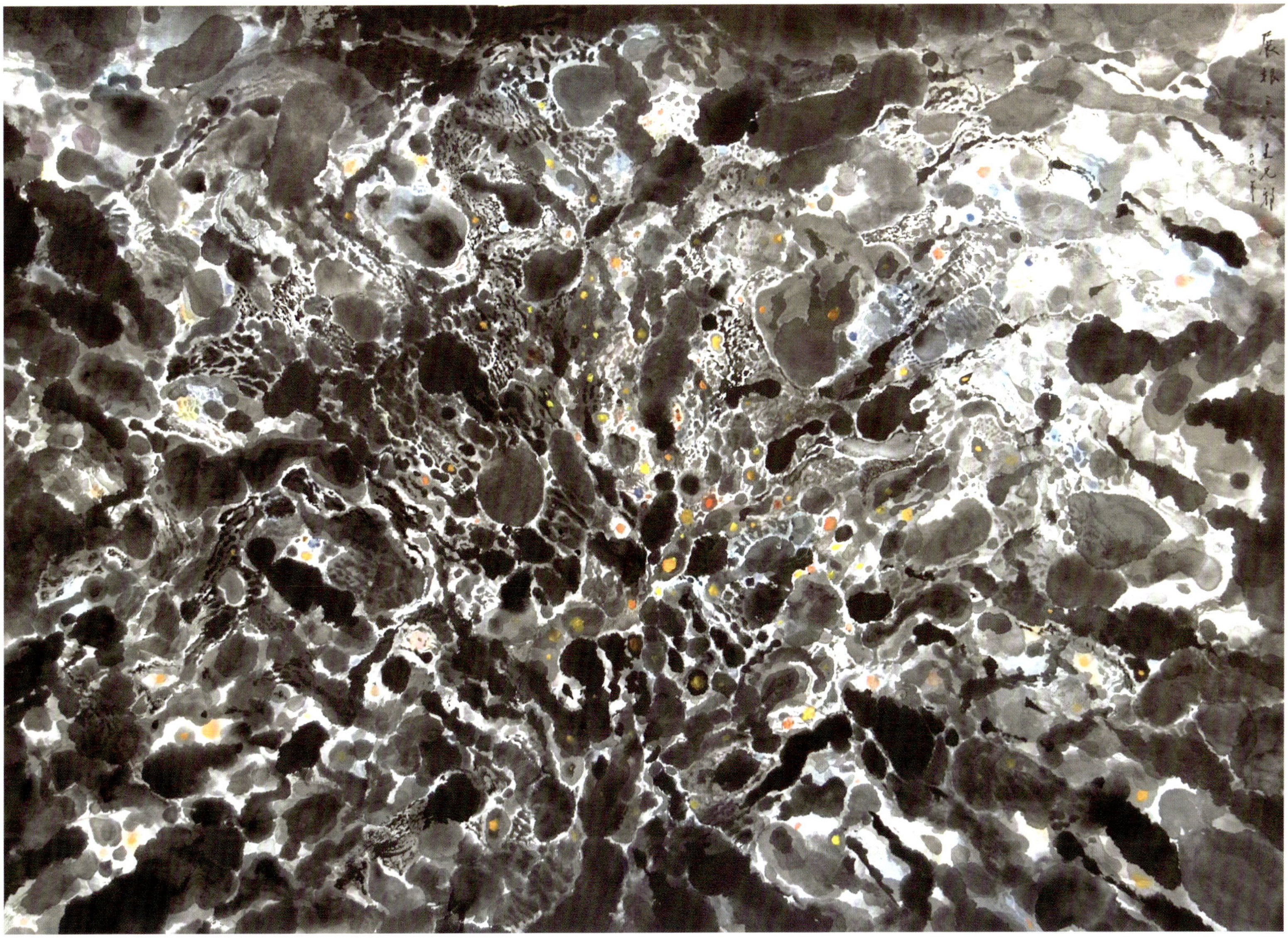

Roots and branches radiate in an abstract composition.
根與枝形成抽象化的構圖。

Spreading The Roots #8
展根之八
Ink,Watercolour and Acrylic on Paper
64 x 91.5 cm, 2008

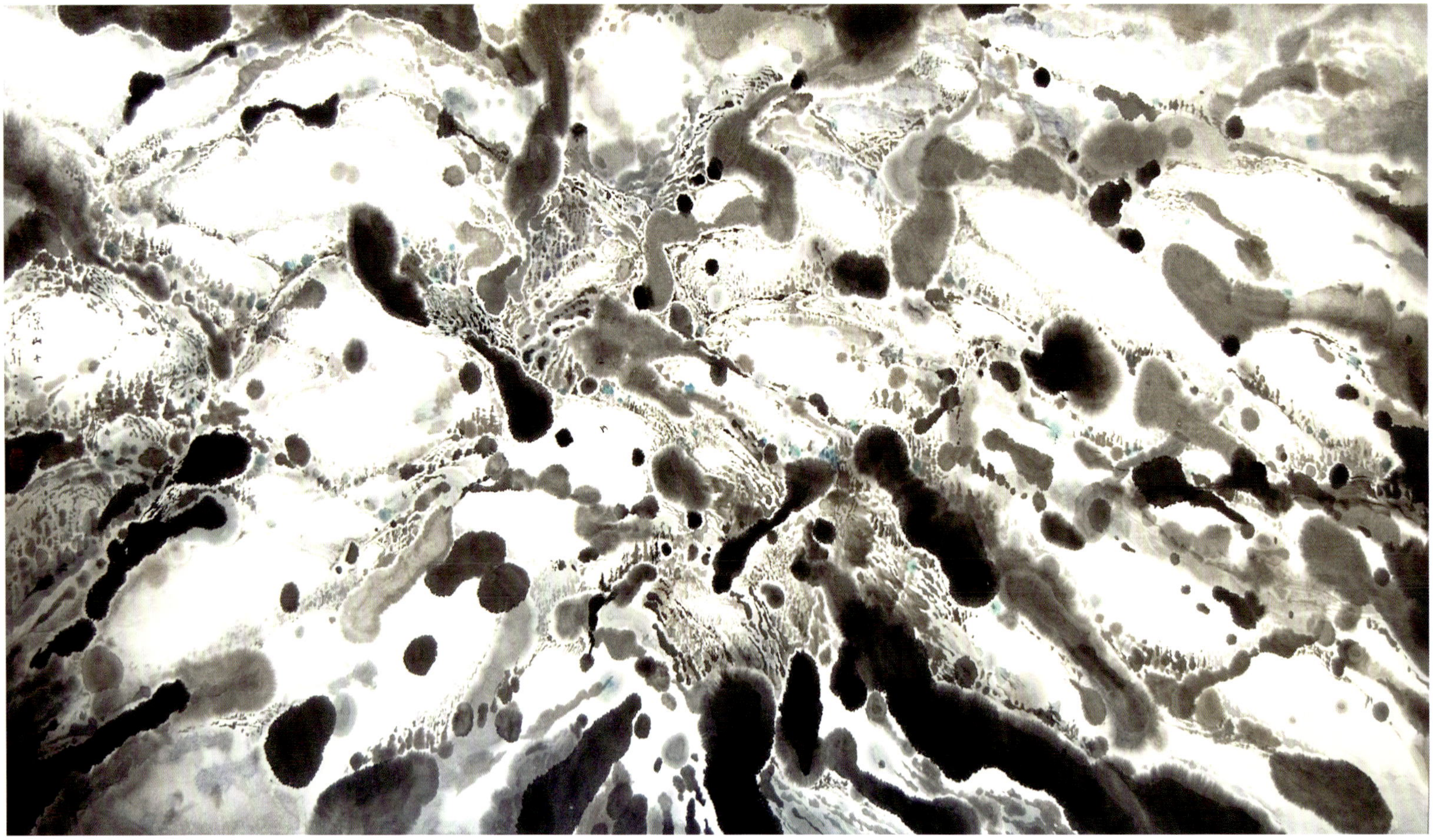

No peak. No sky. Scanty vegetation. Snow hides part of the slopes. This is cold season. Deep in the mountains, tranquility prevails.

山峰沒有在畫面出現。天空也沒有出現。山坡上有雪覆蓋。這是寒冷的季節。山中一片幽寂。

Deep In The Mountains #11
深山十一
Ink,Watercolour and Acrylic on Paper
67 x 117.5 cm, 2008

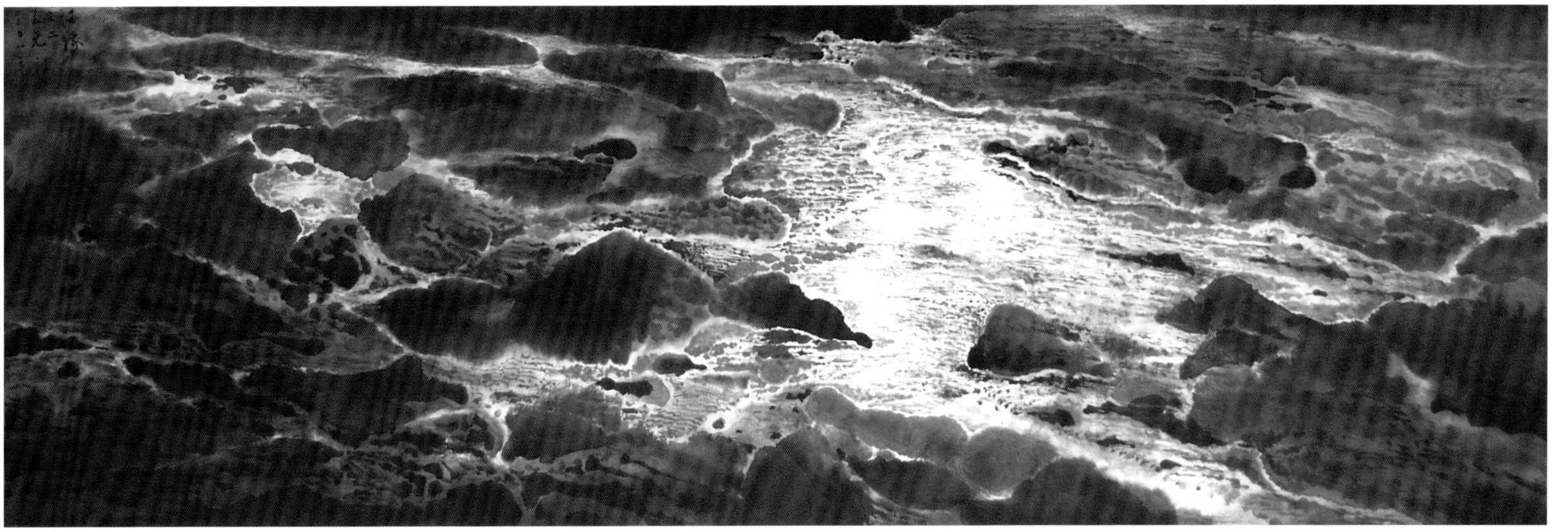

Away from the bustle-hustle, at the end of a working day, city dwellers might find a moment of quietude and relaxation nearby the seashore. Waves wash the fringing rocks. The sun gradually sinks down the horizon. Fading light flickers on the water surface.

營役終日之後，海濱成為城居者暫憩之處。波浪湧洗岸邊石群，太陽緩緩在地平線下沉，餘光在水面閃爍。

Edge Of Sea #2
海緣之二
Ink,Watercolour and Acrylic on Paper
30.5 x 94.5 cm, 2008

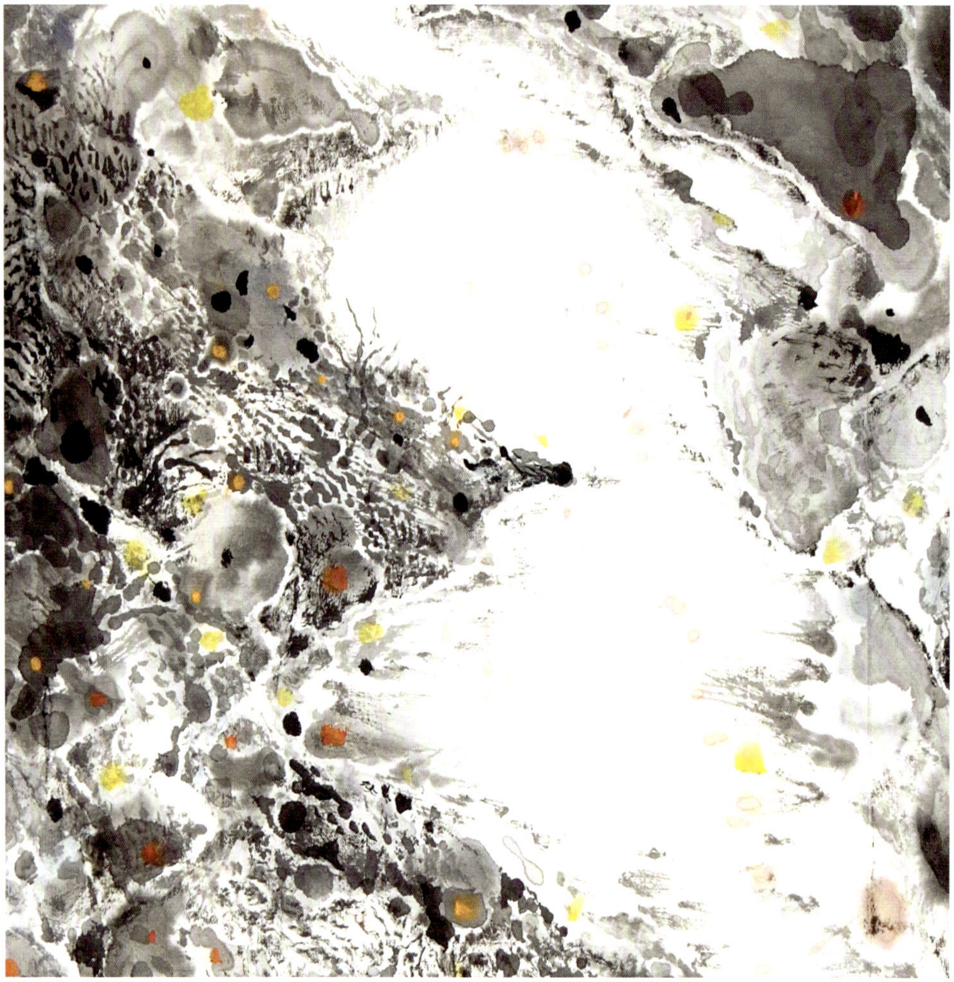

Partial detail of the right
局部細節(右)

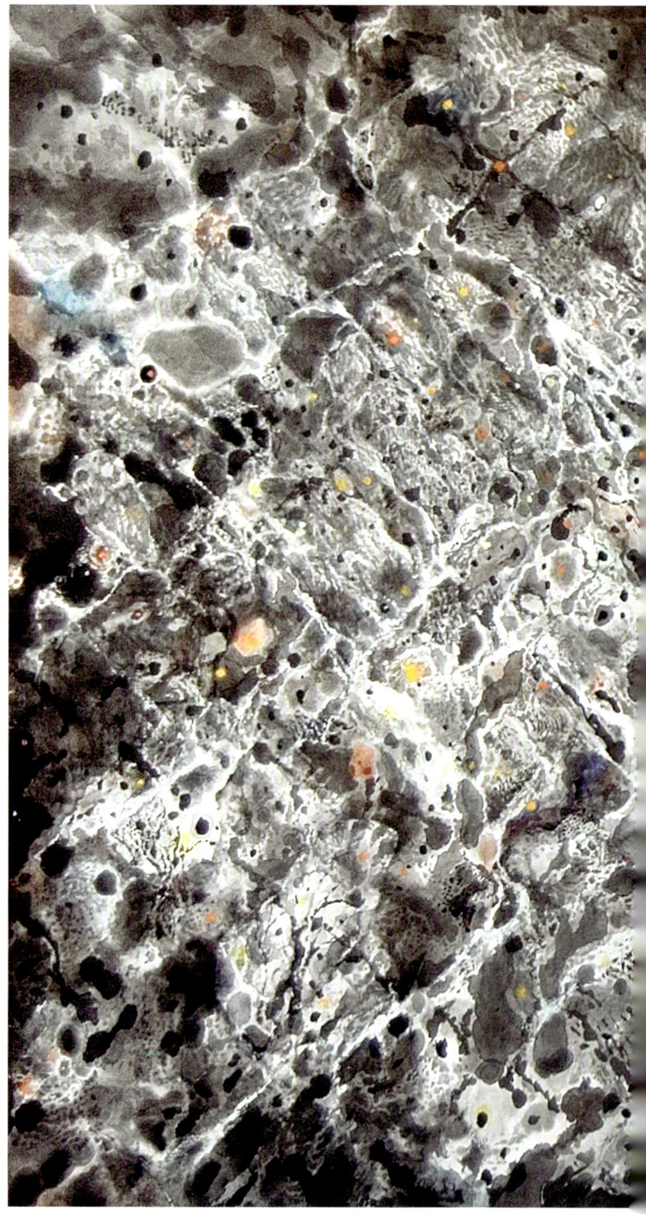

Autumn River
秋江
Ink,Watercolour and Acrylic on Paper
68.5 x 138.5 cm, 2008

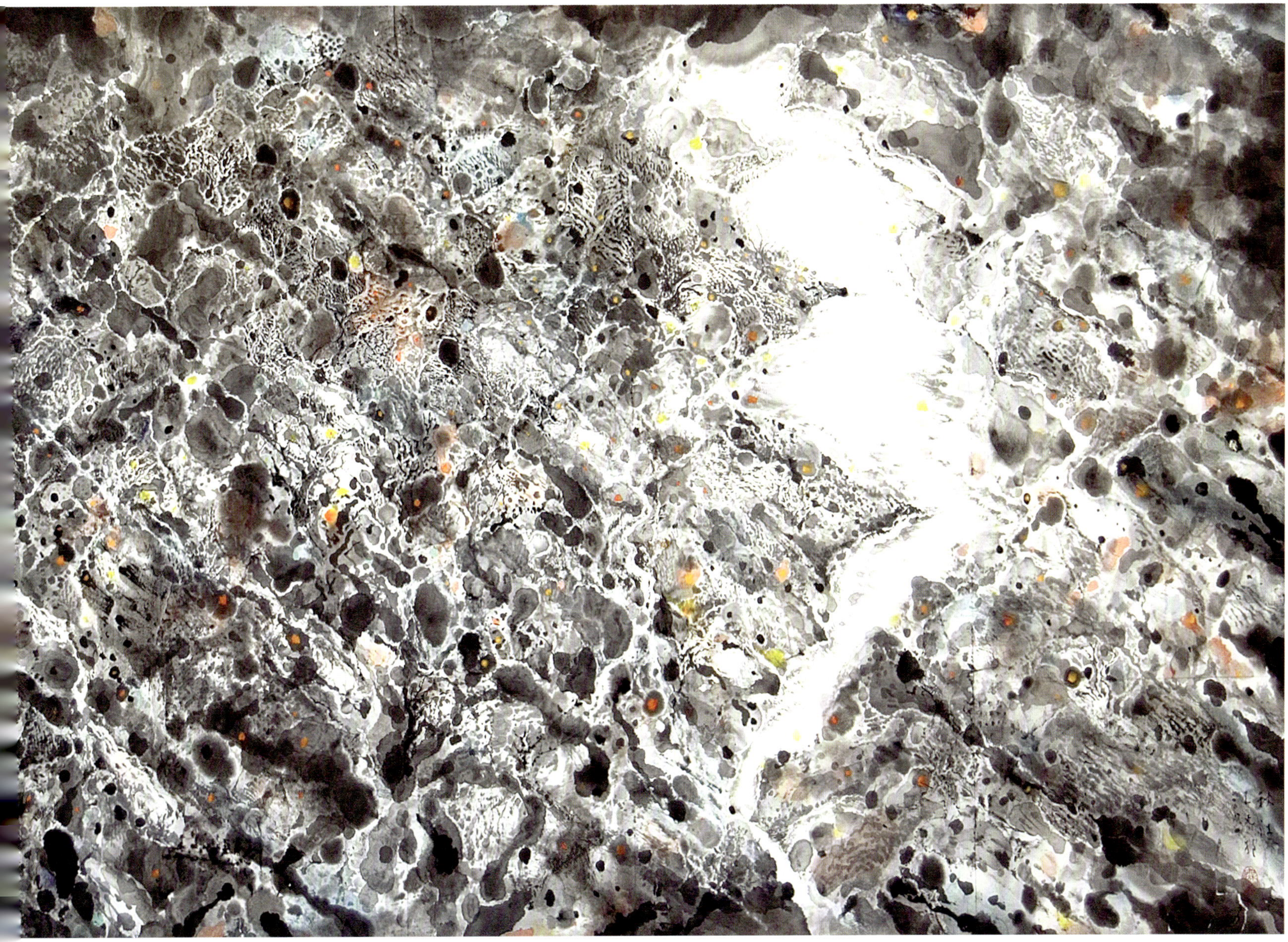

A calm river splits the land. Forest in the southern country never sheds all the leaves. Scattered reddened leaves signify that Autumn is here.

平靜的江水，分開了兩岸。南國的林木，仍然相當茂盛。疏疏幾點的紅葉，稍帶來默默的秋意。

Partial detail of the centre
局部細節（中）

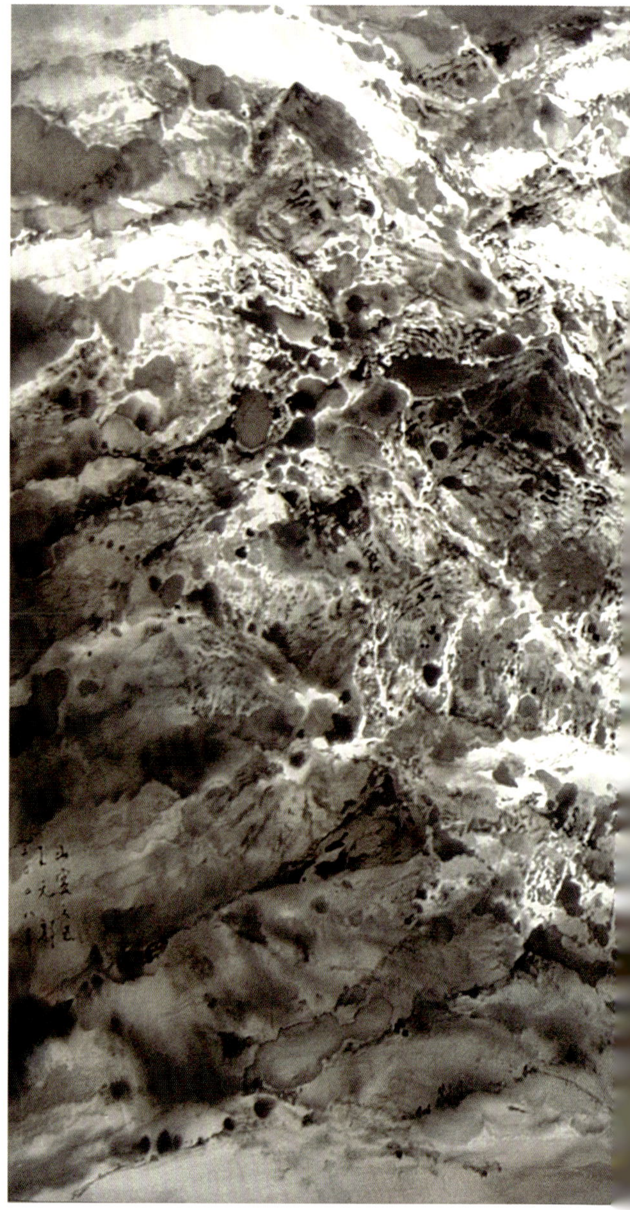

Mountain Clouds #5
山雲之五
Ink,Watercolour and Acrylic on Paper
61 x 123 cm, 2008

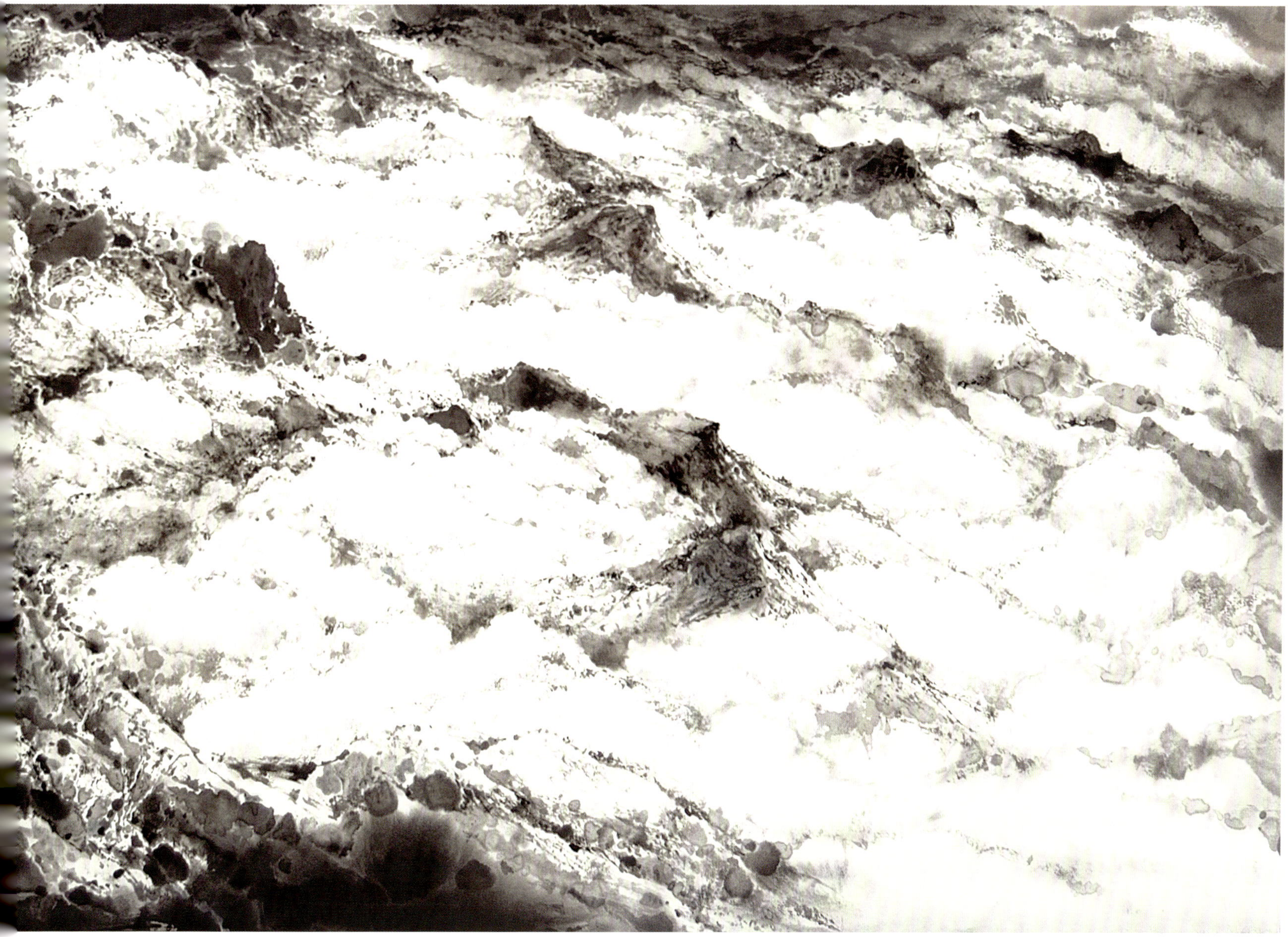

Mountain acquires solidity with light and shade, and animated with moving clouds that conceal and veil its different parts. Clouds are represented by leaving blank areas on the paper, by they are actually white masses with noticeable shapes. The presence of clouds offers wider breathable space expressing a feeling of sublimity.

光影塑出山之軀體。雲可表現山之動感。雲有厚薄，厚如棉球可掩部分山形，薄如輕紗可使山形出沒在有無之間。以水墨畫雲，留白為上。雲，可給予畫面有較大的呼吸的空間，引致空靈感或超脫感。

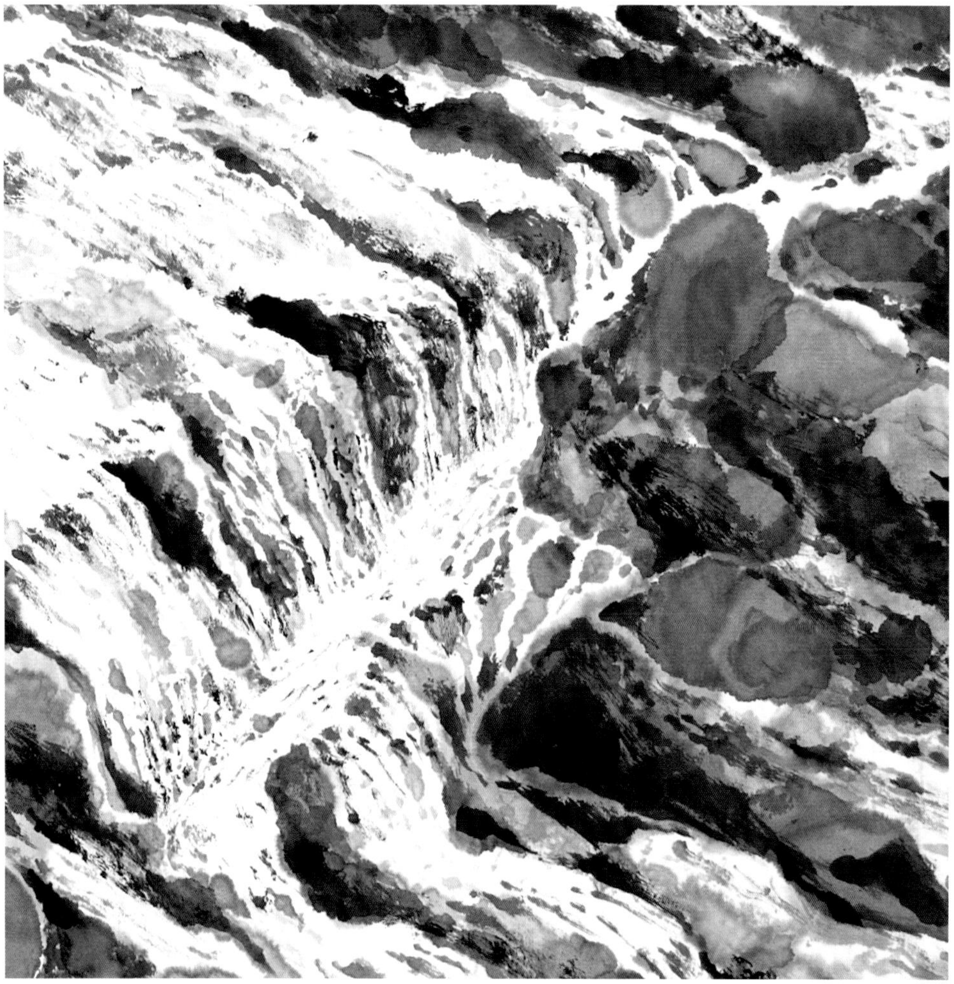

Partial detail of the right
局部細節(右)

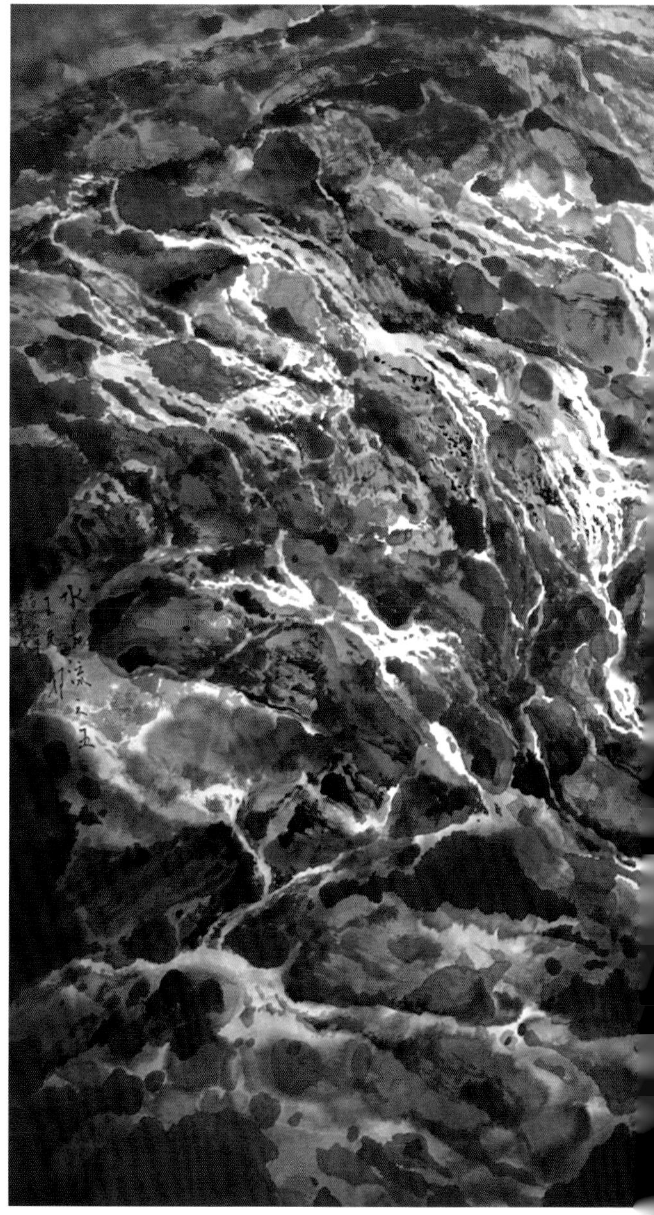

Running Water Forever #5
水長流之五
Ink,Watercolour and Acrylic on Paper
61 x 123 cm, 2008

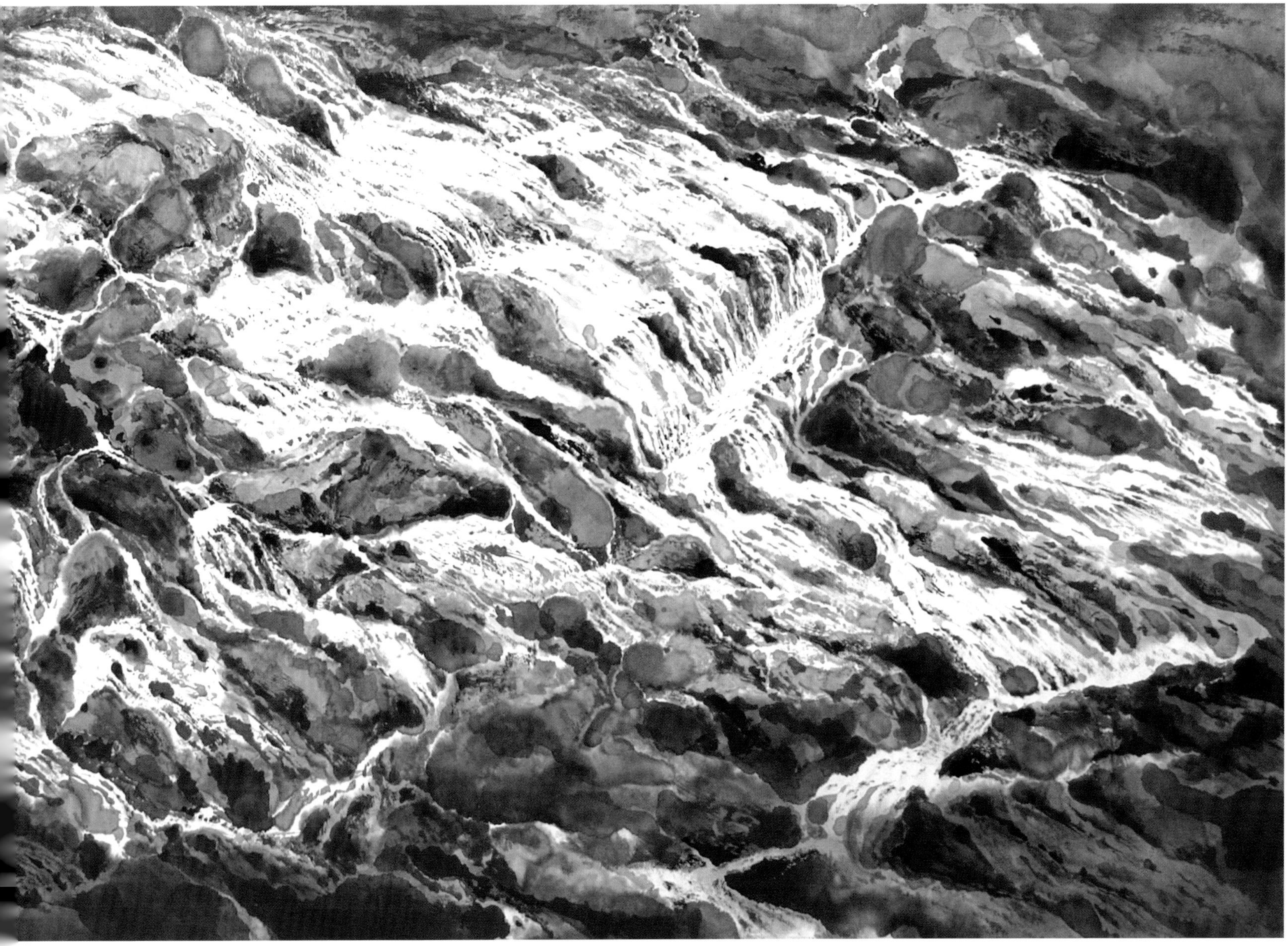

Nature engenders life. Life never stops. Water drips and sprouts, jumps and rushes, in an everlasting momentum. This painting portrays water moving among rocks, jumping in steps as it diverges and converges rhythmically with varying speeds, forming a wide net on the land.

大自然生生不息，流水涓涓，其源不竭。此作近寫清泉石上流，逐層下躍，散聚分合，緩速有致，有如巨網。

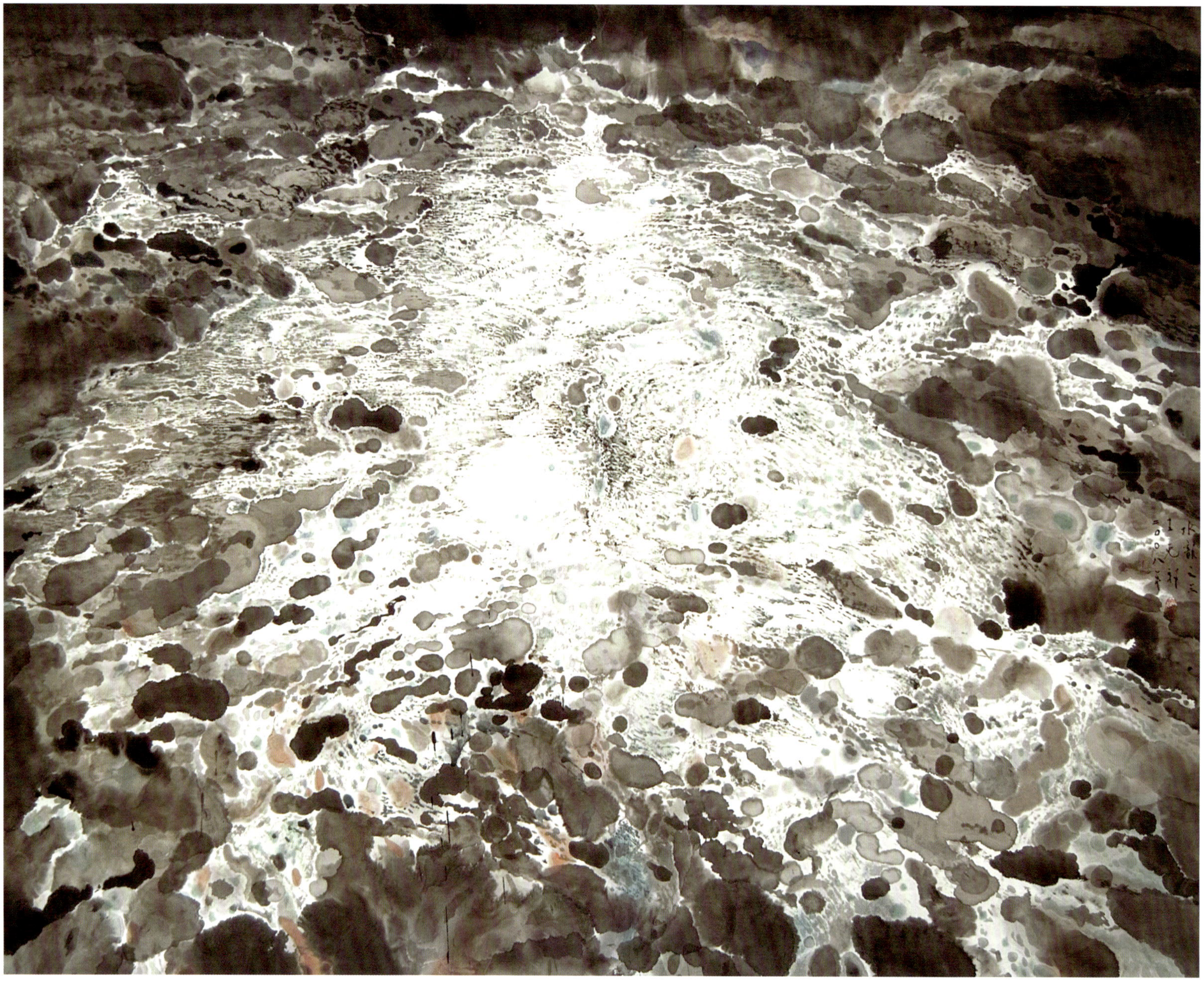

Recently I moved the southern part of the Hong Kong Island, and have a broad view of the sea greeting my eyes everyday. On fine days, white clouds and evening mist enliven my heart. The sea receives rivers from all directions as it has immense capacity. As I paint this, I am able to release myself from the over-crowded environment.

近遷港島南區，常見遼闊海面，晴天朗日，朝雲晚霞，都使心胸開揚。海納百川，有容乃大，因想到寫海，衝出受困擾的擠逼空間。

Water Melody #3
水韻之三
Ink,Watercolour and Acrylic on Paper
95 x 123 cm, 2008

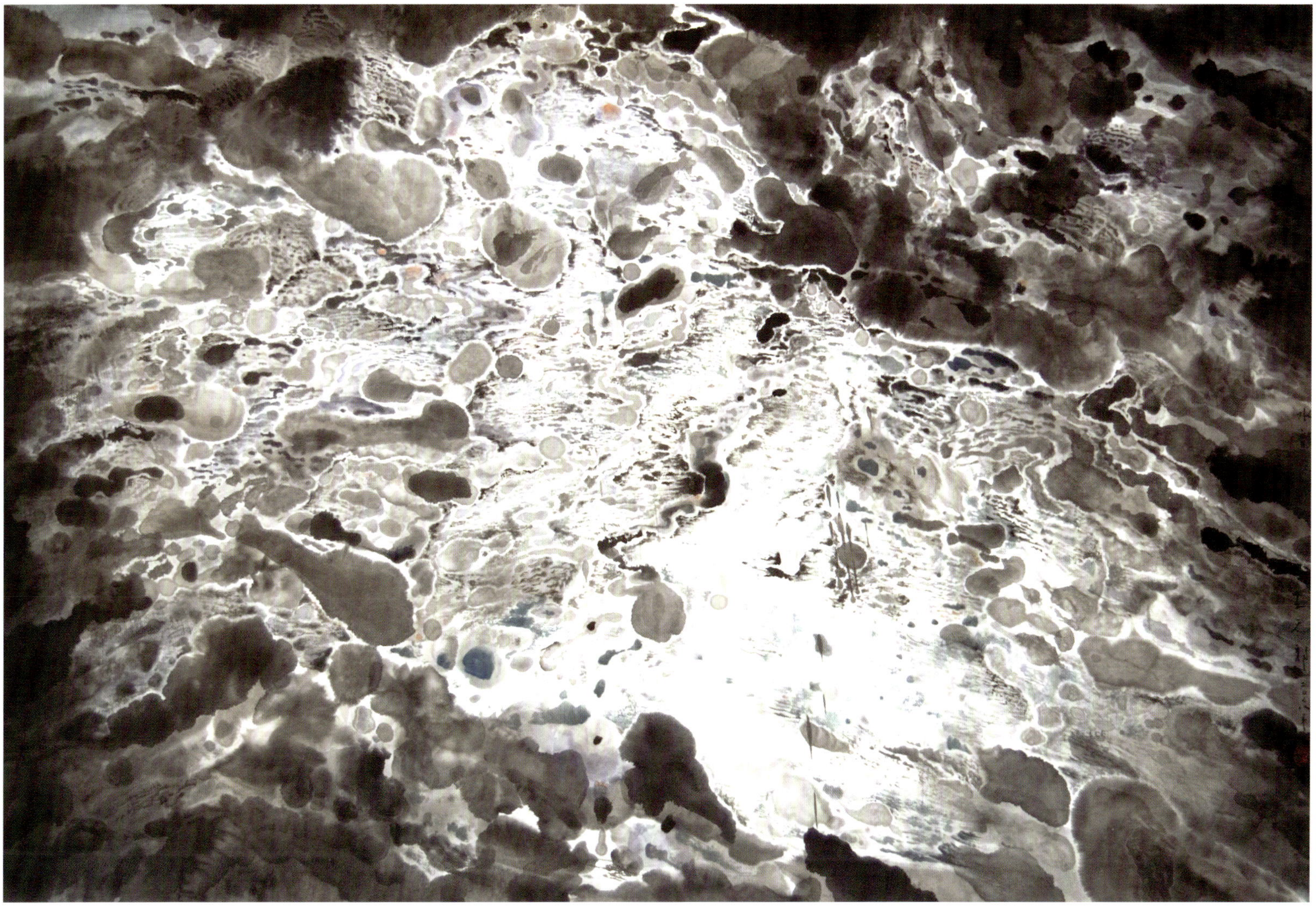

The sea reflects light from above. Land may still form a backdrop to the sea, but it is no longer significant. Patterns on the water are made with waves and light, and change from moment to moment to delight the eyes.

海面反射天上的光。陸地仍然是水之涯，不過只是無關重要的背景。水紋由波浪與光之反映構成，瞬息萬變，令人心曠神怡。

Water Melody #5
水韻之五
Ink,Watercolour and Acrylic on Paper
84 x 123 cm, 2008

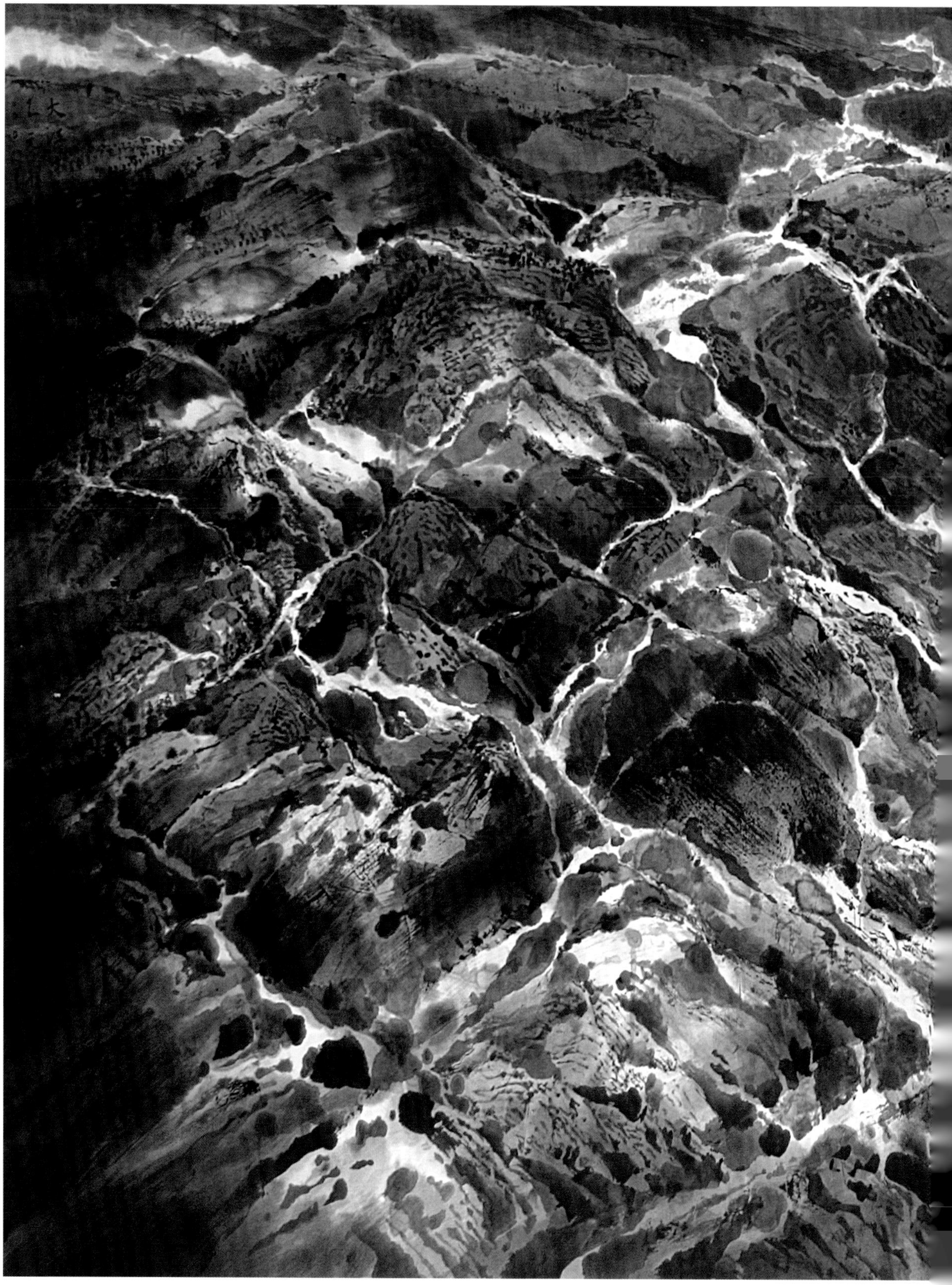

Great River #15
大江十五
Ink,Watercolour and Acrylic on Paper
95 x 176 cm, 2008

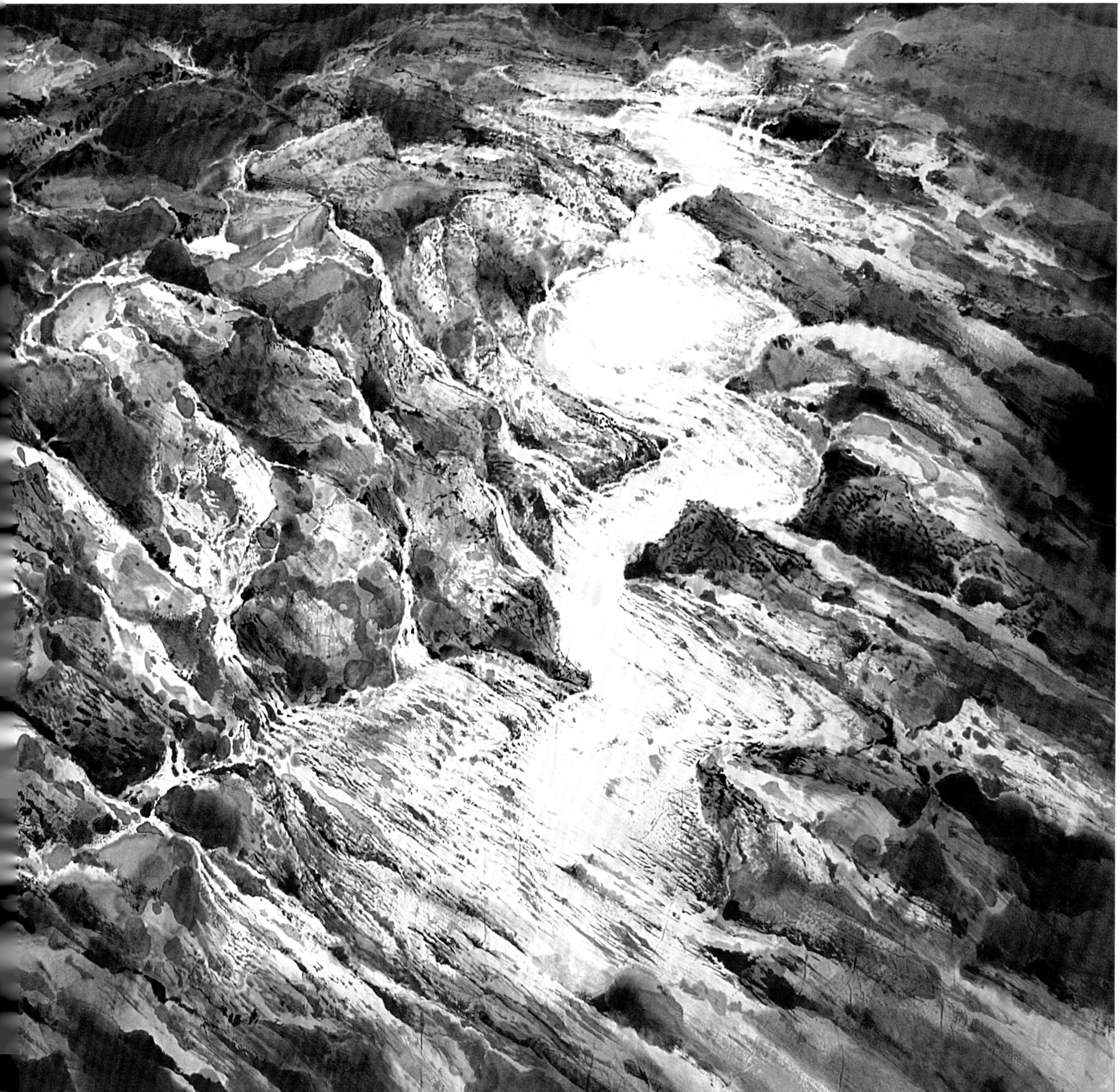

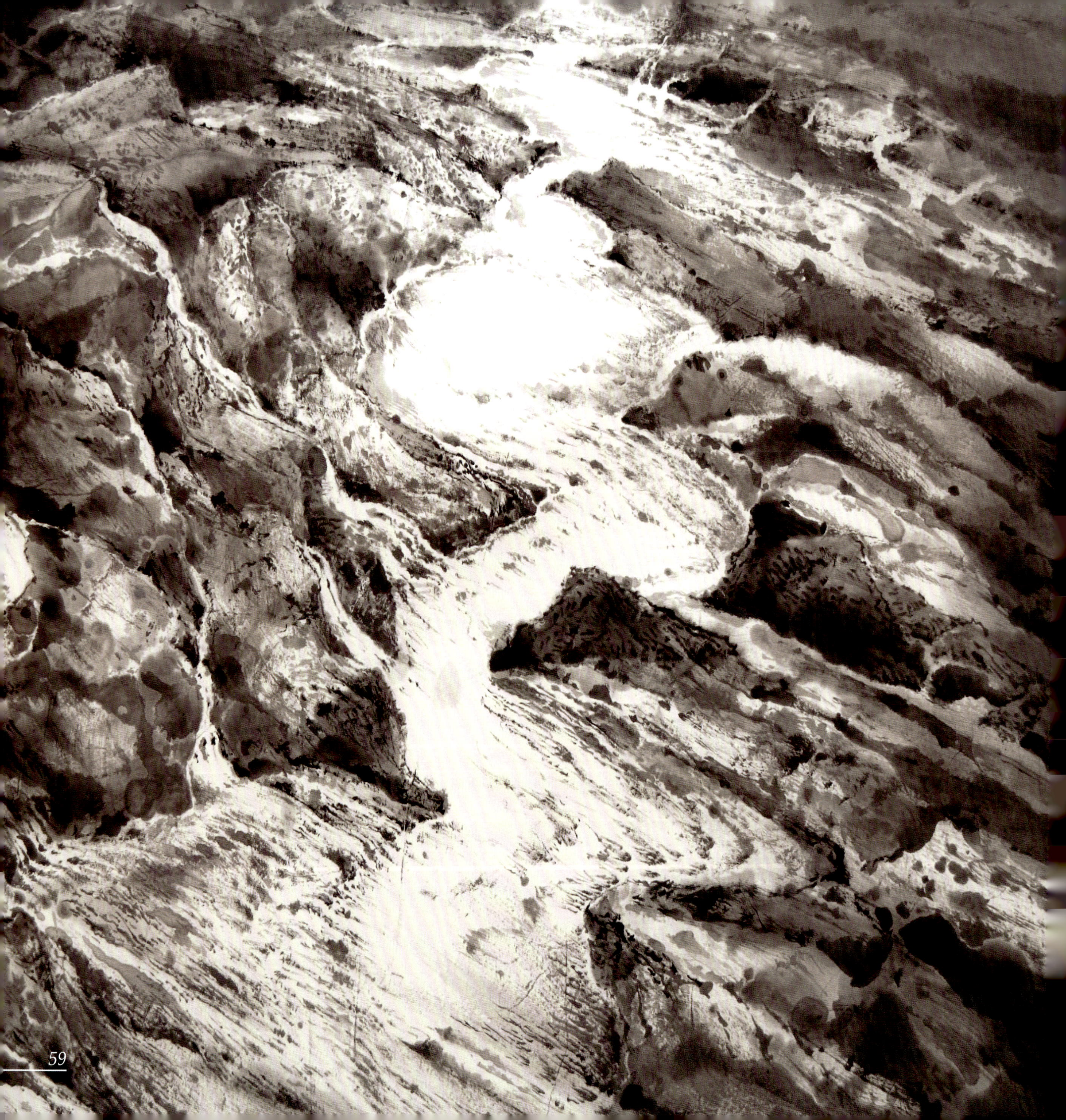

From a high viewpoint, this magnificent river winds forward. It will reach the distant sea and will never return (poem by Bai Juyi). The river has become a favourite theme among many poets and essayists. The source of the river lies in the remote distance, but not beyond reach. I have always had a deep feeling for rivers. China is a civilization associated with rivers. I was born on the bank of the Pearl River, and is now residing closely to its delta.

登高壯觀天地間，大江茫茫去不還（白居易詩句）。江水東流，一直是詩人墨客筆下的慨嘆。水之源頭，遠在天邊，今日非不可尋達。大江於我，有一種深厚感情。中國本來是江河文化的國家。我來自珠江，現住近珠江的出口。

Partial detail of the right, Great River #15
大江十五局部細節（右）

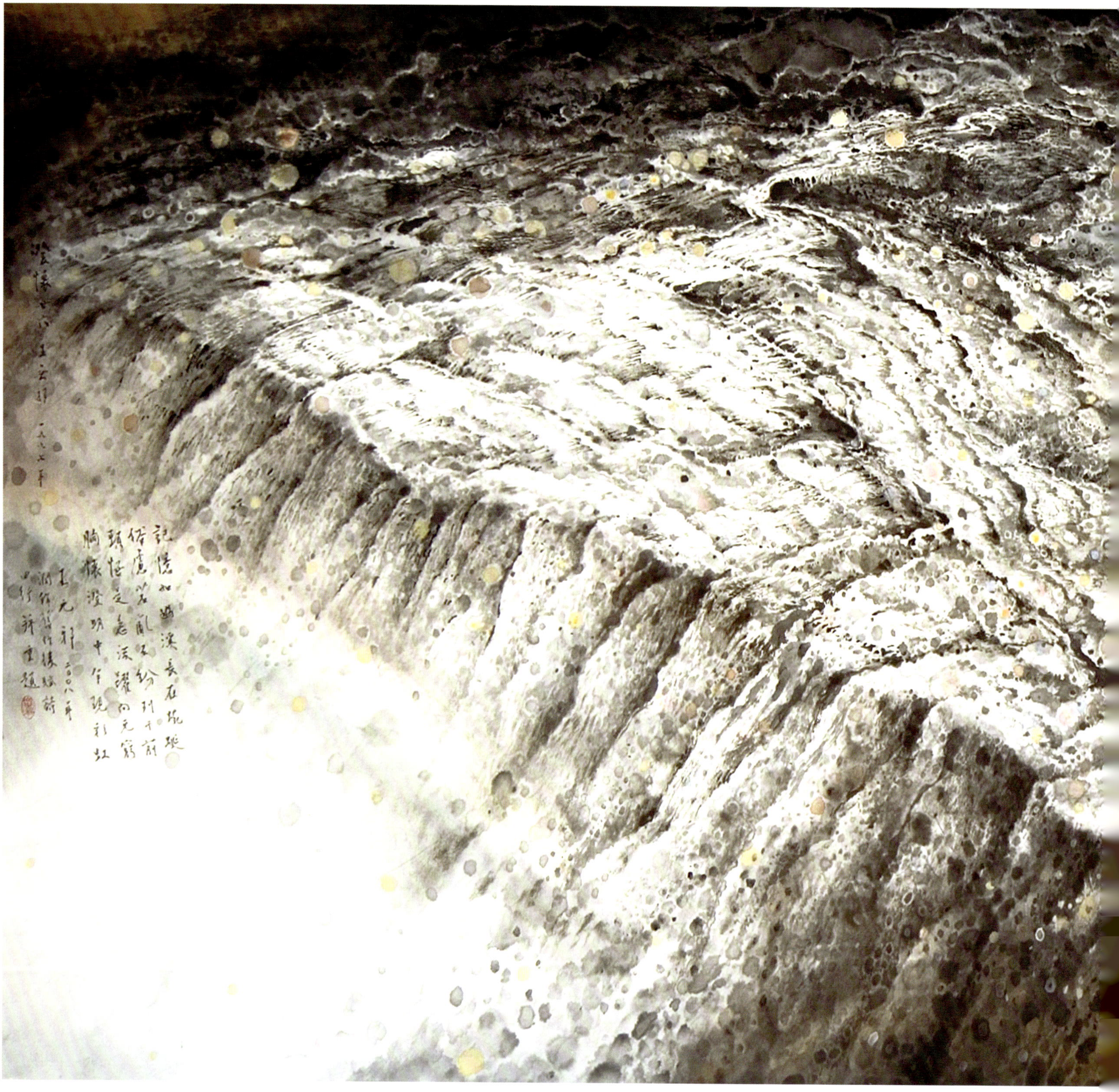

Meditation #26
澄懷廿六
Ink,Watercolour and Acrylic on Paper
96.5 x 212 cm, 2008

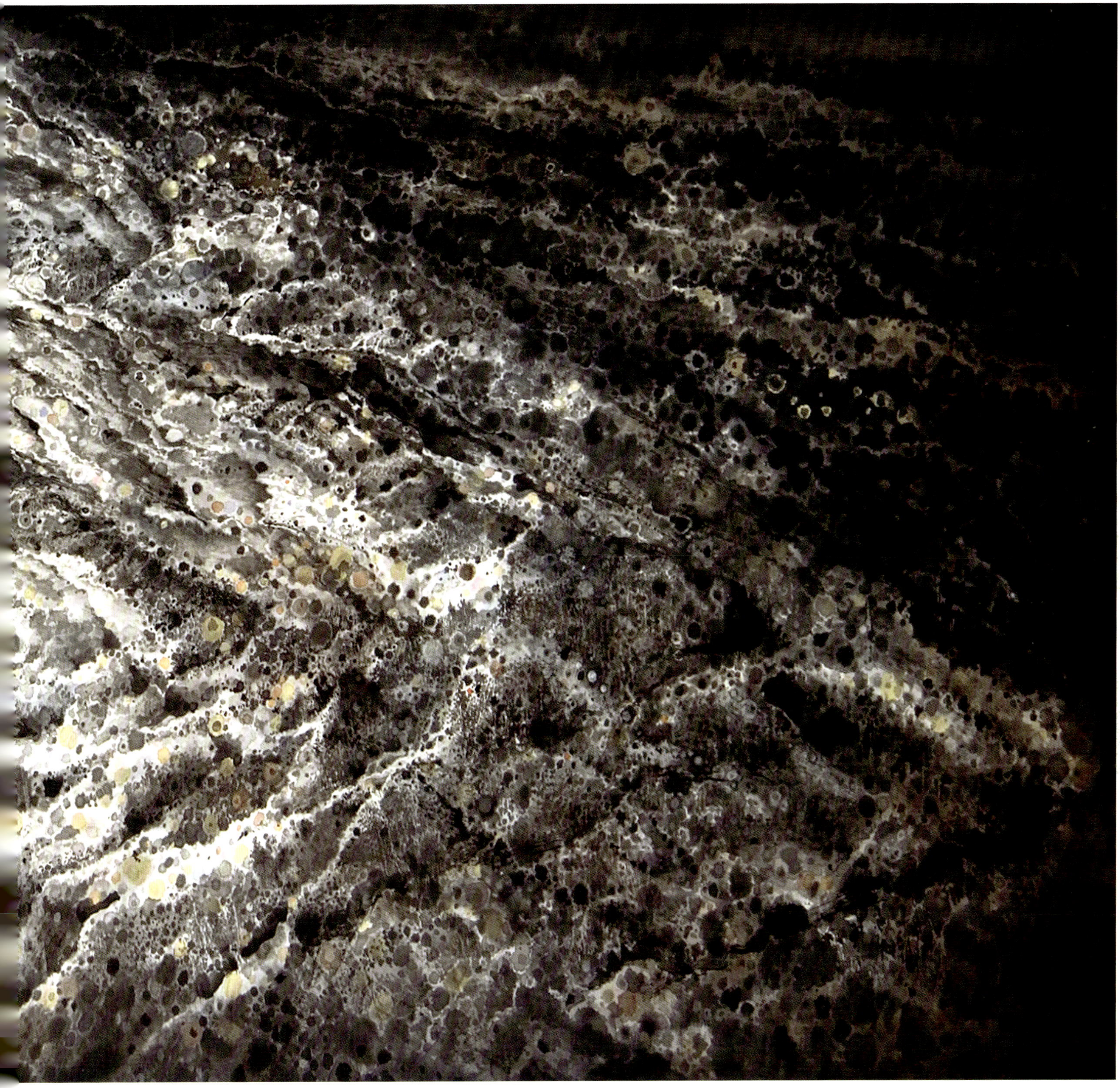

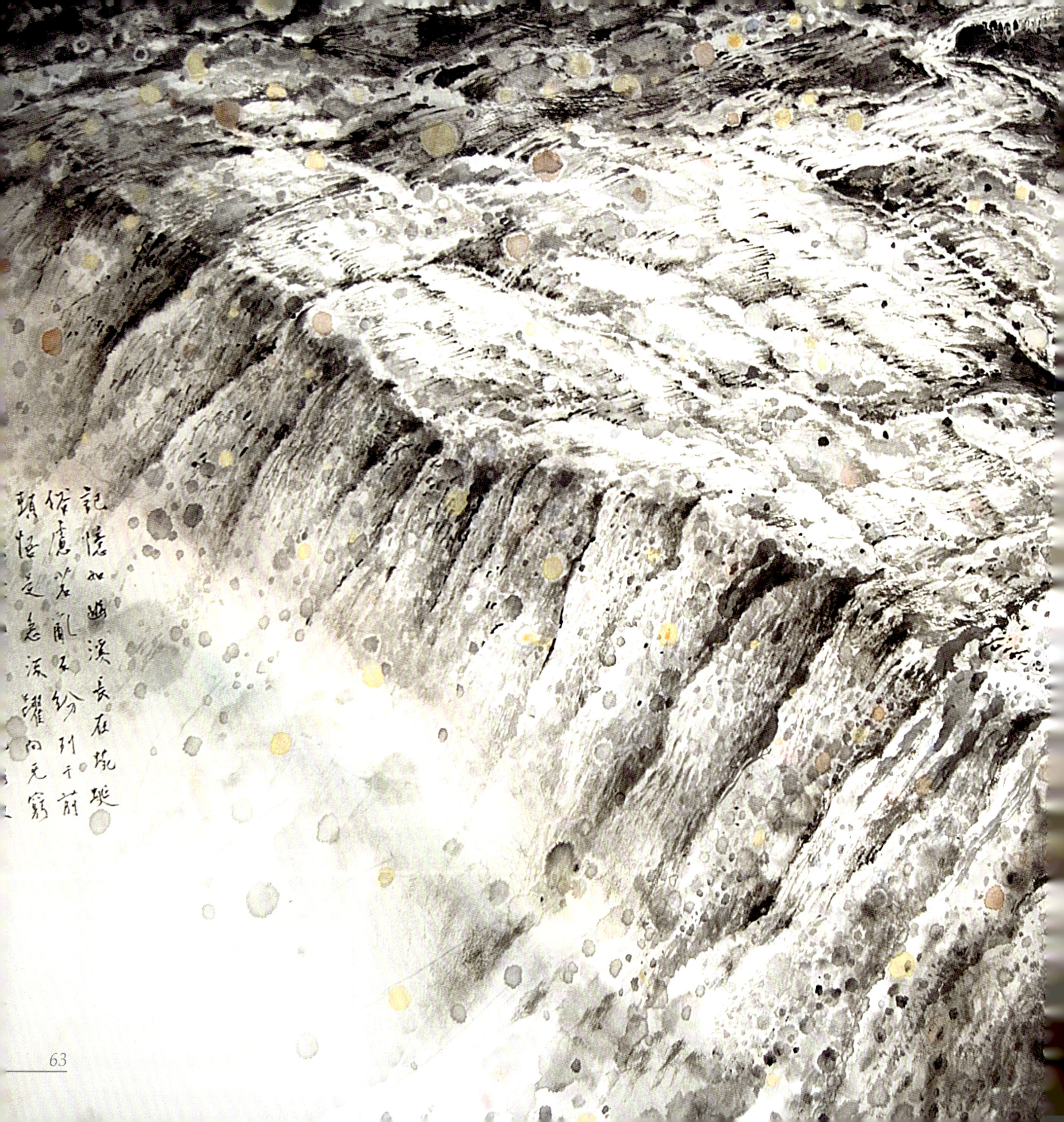
記憶如幽溪長在坑壑
依舊若亂石紛列于前
頓悟是急流躍向無窮

The series of paintings entitled "Meditation" was inspired by memories of the Nigara Falls. Facing the immense forces of Nature one can withdraw more to inner world with all vulgar thoughts washed away.

"澄懷"是一系列作品表現尼亞加拉大瀑布的總題。大自然宏偉力量之展示，使我們俗慮盡消，尋回內心的澄明。

Memory lingers as a quietly winding stream
Vulgar thoughts are the rocks scattering all over
Water suddenly plunges into enlightenment
In meditation a rainbow emerges from my heart

記憶如幽溪長在蜿蜒
俗慮若亂石紛列于前
頓悟是急流躍向無窮
胸懷澄明中乍現彩虹

Partial detail of the left, Meditation #26
澄懷廿六局部細節(左)

BIOGRAPHY

傳略

SELECTED SOLO EXHIBITIONS

1959 The British Council, Hong Kong
1979 Paintings Drawings Prints, City Museum and Art Gallery, Hong Kong
1986 Charlotte Horstmann & Gerald Godfrey, Hong Kong
1987 Mountain Thoughts, Minneapolis Institute of Arts, Minnesota
1989 River Dreams, Gerald Godfrey Far Eastern Art, London
Water and Clouds, Hanart Gallery, New York
1992 The East-West Journey, Hsiung Shih Gallery, Taipei
Ancient Dreams, Godfrey Far Eastern Art, London
1994 New Paintings, Hanart T.Z. Gallery, Hong Kong
1997 Visions of a Wanderer, Plum Blossoms International, Hong Kong and Singapore
1998 Ring of Fire, Kaikodo Gallery, New York
1999 Eastern Moods, Western Modes, Works on Canvas, Hanart T.Z. Gallery, Hong Kong
2000 Goedhuis Contemporary, London
2002 City Dreams, Works on Paper and Fabric, Hanart T.Z. Gallery, Hong Kong
2004 Window Dreams, Grotto Fine Arts, Hong Kong
2006 At the East-West Crossroads, Retrospective Exhibition, Hong Kong Museum of Art, Hong Kong
2008 Spirit of Sky and Land, iPreciation, Singapore

SELECTED GROUP EXHIBITIONS

1960 First International Salon of Paintings, Hong Kong
1961 Sao Paulo Biennale, Sao Paulo, Brazil
1964 Annual Exhibition, Baltimore Museum of Art, Maryland
1971 Art Now Hong Kong, organized by City Museum and Art Gallery
travelled to London, Bristol, Edinburgh, & Manchester
1972 Contemporary Hong Kong Art, Pacificulture Museum, Pasadena, California
1982 First Exhibition of Asian Art, Bahrain
1983 Overseas Chinese Artists Exhibition, Taipei Fine Arts Museum, Taiwan
1984 Centennial Collection: Masterpieces for Minnesota, Minneapolis Institute of Arts, Minnesota
1985 A Selection of Twentieth Century Chinese Painting, Art Gallery of Greater Victoria, BC, Canada
1986 Development of Modern Chinese Painting: Retrospective Exhibition, Taipei Fine Arts Museum
1987 Chinese Paintings: Traces of the Brush, Minnesota Museum of Art, St. Paul, Minnesota
1988 Continuity and Change: Five Contemporary Chinese Artists, Yale University Art Gallery, New Haven
First International Ink Painting Exhibition, Beijing
1992 Second International Ink Painting Exhibition, Shenzhen
Contemporary Works from the Hong Kong Museum of Art, Vancouver Art Gallery, Canada
1993 Visions in Between: Paintings by Chinese, Japanese and Korean Artists, Ise Foundation, New York
Summer Exhibition, Royal Academy of Arts, London
1994 Beyond the Borders, Bronx Museum of the Arts, New York
1996 Mutations of Ink and Paper, Exhibition of Works by Chinese-American Artists on the East Coast, New York
Tradition and Innovation - Twentieth Century Chinese Painting, Hong Kong Museum of Art, travelled to Singapore Art Museum, British Museum, and Museum fur Ostasiatische Kunst, Koln, Germany
1997 Hong Kong Art 1997 Exhibition, National Art Gallery, Beijing, and Guangdong Art Museum, Guangzhou

個展選錄

1959 英國文化協會，香港
1979 繪畫 素描 版畫，香港博物館美術館
1986 葛富利畫廊，香港
1987 山之情懷，明尼亞玻里市藝術館
1989 河夢，葛富利畫廊，倫敦
水意雲情，漢雅軒，紐約
1992 東西行，雄獅畫廊，台北
故夢，葛富利畫廊，倫敦
1994 新作展，漢雅軒，香港
1997 遊子情懷，萬玉堂畫廊，香港及新加玻
1998 火之環，懷古堂，紐約
1999 東夢西尋，油畫作品展，漢雅軒，香港
2000 顧豪斯當代畫廊，倫敦
2002 城夢，漢雅軒，香港
2004 窗夢集，嘉圖畫廊，香港
2006 東西問道，回顧展，香港藝術館，香港
2008 天地情懷，誰先覺畫廊，新加坡

聯展選錄

1960 首屆香港國際繪畫沙龍
1961 聖保羅國際美術雙年展，巴西
1964 巴爾鐵摩美術館年展，美國馬利蘭州
1971 今日香港藝術，香港博物美術館主辦，巡迴英國倫敦、比利斯圖、曼徹斯特、愛丁堡
1972 當代香港藝術展，太平洋文化博物館，加州巴薩甸納
1982 首屆亞洲藝術大展，中東巴林
1984 創館百年紀念藏品精選展，明尼蘇達美術館
1985 二十世紀中國繪畫，維多利亞美術館，加拿大卑詩省
1986 當代中國繪畫，香港中文大學文物館
1988 古色今香，華裔畫家五人展，耶魯大學美術館，康涅狄克州
1992 第二屆國際水墨畫展，深圳
1993 紐約亞裔藝術家聯展，巡迴紐約、台北、台中、高雄、韓國漢城、日本福岡美術館展出
夏季大展，倫敦皇家藝術學會
1994 沒有邊界的藝術，紐約布朗士藝術館
1996 紙墨變奏：美東華人藝術家作品展，紐約中華新聞文化中心
傳統與創新：現代中國畫展，香港藝術館、新加坡美術館、大英博物館、哥隆東方美術館
1997 香港藝術一九九七展，北京中國美術館及廣州廣東美術館
亞洲傳統，現代表現，新澤西州立大學美術館，巡迴紐約、芝加哥、台北、日本及韓國
1998 中華五千年文明藝術大展，紐約古庚漢美術館
上海雙年展，上海美術館
2000 共慶回歸祖國一中國藝術大展，澳門藝術博物館
二十世紀中國油畫大展，中國美術館，北京
2001 當代中國美術，蘇立文伉儷藏品展，英國牛津亞殊慕連美術館

Asian Traditions/Modern Expressions: Asian American Artists and Abstraction, 1945-1970, Jane Voorhees Zimmerli Art Museum, Rutgers, State University of New Jersey, New Brunswick, New Jersey

1998 China, 5000 Years Innovation and Transformation in the Arts, Guggenheim Museum, New York
Shanghai Biennial, Shanghai Art Museum

2000 Exposi de Arte Chiesa Celebra do regresso de Macau Pria , Museu de Arte de Macau
Twentieth Century Chinese Oil Painting Exhibition, National Art Gallery, Beijing

2001 Contemporary Chinese Art from the Khoan and Michael Sullivans Collection, Ashmolean Museum, Oxford, U.K.

2002 Second International Ink Painting Biennial, Shenzhen
Hong Kong Cityscapes Ink Painting in Transition, presented by the Hong Kong Museum of Art at the Hong Kong Festival in London

2003 Third Nationwide Oil Painting Exhibition, China Art Gallery, Beijing

2004 Ink Painting Triennial, Jiangxu Art Museum, Nanjing
Third International Ink Painting Biennial, Shenzhen

2006 Contemporary Hong Kong Ink Painting Exhibition, Hong Kong and Shenzhen
Contemporary Ink Painting, Do Lun Art Museum, Shanghai

2007 Chinese Artists Painting Xinjiang, National Art Gallery, Beijing
China Onward, Chinese Contemporary Art, Louisiana Museum of Modern Art, Denmark

2008 Asian Traditions/Modern Expressions, de Young Museum, San Francisco
New Ink Art: Innovation and Beyond, Hong Kong Museum of Art
2008 Olympic Arts Collection, International Exhibition Centre, Beijing
One World, Chinese Paintings of the UN Family by Chinese Artists, Geneva, New York and other cities
Joint Exhibition of Shenzhen and Hong Kong Artists, Shenzhen and Hong Kong

MURAL COMMISSIONS

1982 Mural for the A & M University, Tallahassee, Florida, commissioned by the Chase Manhattan Bank

1998 Mural for the Kerry Centre, Shanghai, commissioned by the Kerry Group, Hong Kong

1999 Mural for the Regal Airport Hotel, Chek Lap Kok, commissioned by the Paliburg Group, Hong Kong

AWARDS

1970 John D. Rockefeller III Fund Grant

1998 Emeritus Fellowship, Hong Kong Arts Development Council

2007 Bronze Bauhinia Medal, Hong Kong SAR Government

SELECTED COLLECTIONS

American Express
Arthur M. Sackler Museum, Harvard University
Art Institute of Chicago
Ashmolean Museum, Oxford, UK
Asian Art Museum, San Francisco
British Museum
Chase Manhattan Bank
City University of New York
Heritage Museum, Hong Kong
Hong Kong & Shanghai Banking Corporation

2002 第二屆深圳國際水墨畫雙年展

2003 第三屆全國油畫展，中國美術館，北京

2004 南京水墨畫三年展，江蘇美術館，南京
第三屆深圳國際水墨畫雙年展

2006 香港當代水墨畫大展，香港及深圳
中港台水墨畫展，多倫美術館，上海

2007 中國畫 畫中國 走進新疆，中國美術館，北京
中國邁步，當代中國藝術展，路易士安納現代美術館，丹麥

2008 亞洲傳統 現代表現，德揚美術館，美國三藩市
新水墨藝術一創造、超越、翱翔，香港藝術館
2008奧林匹克美術大會，中國國際展覽中心，北京
同一個世界，中國畫家彩繪聯合國大家庭藝術大展，巡迴日內瓦、紐約及其他各地
深港水墨畫交流展，深圳畫院及香港中央圖書館

壁畫製作

1982 美國大通銀行委託，為美國佛羅里達州泰拉哈西市A&M大學繪製壁畫

1998 香港嘉里集團委託，為上海嘉里中心大堂繪製壁畫

1999 香港百利保集團委託，為香港富豪機場酒店接待大堂繪製壁畫

獎 項

1970 美國紐約洛克菲勒三世基金會藝術研究獎助

1998 香港藝術發展局藝術成就獎

2007 香港特區政府頒授銅紫荊勳章

藏家選錄

上海美術館
常州美術館
英國大英博物館
英國牛津亞殊慕連美術館
美國波士頓美術館
美國芝加哥美術館
美國明尼亞玻里市藝術館
美國明尼蘇達美術館
美國運通銀行
美國市立紐約大學
美國大通銀行
美國摩根信託銀行
美國普天壽保險公司
美國聯合航空公司
美國世界銀行
美國哈佛大學薩克勒美術館
美國三藩市亞洲美術館
德國柏林東方美術館
香港藝術館
香港文化博物館

Hong Kong Jockey Club
Hong Kong Land
Hong Kong Museum of Art
Hong Kong Polytechnic University
Minneapolis Institute of Arts
Minnesota Museum of Art
Morgan Guaranty Trust
Museum of Fine Arts, Boston
Museum fur Ostasiatische Kunst, Berlin, Germany
National Gallery of Victoria, Melbourne
The Prudential, New York
Shanghai Art Museum
Standard & Chartered Bank
United Airlines
University of Hong Kong
The World Bank

SELECTED PUBLICATIONS

Principles of Two-Dimensional Design
English Edition: Van Nostrand Reinhold, New York, 1972
John Wiley, New York, 1998
Chinese Edition: Hsiung Shih, Taipei, 1980
Spanish Edition: Gustav Gili SA, Barcelona
Indonesian Edition: Penedit ITB, Bandung, 1986

Principles of Color Design
English Edition: Van Nostrand Reinhold, New York, 1987
(Revised and Expanded Edition 1997)
John Wiley, New York, 1998

The Tao of Chinese Landscape Painting
English Edition: Design Press, McGraw-Hill, New York, 1991

Principles of Form and Design
English Edition: Van Nostrand Reinhold, New York, 1993
John Wiley, New York, 1998
Spanish Edition: Gustavo Gili, SA, Barcelona, 1996

Visual Design on the Computer
English Edition: Design Books, Lyons and Burford, New York, 1994
Revised Second Edition, W.W. Norton, New York, 2001

香港大學博物美術館
香港理工大學
香港賽馬會
香港置地有限公司
香港標準渣打銀行
香港匯豐銀行
澳洲墨爾本維多利亞美術館

著作選錄

平面設計原理　英文版，紐約雷恩浩特出版社，1972年
英文版，紐約韋利出版社，1999年
中文版，台北雄獅出版社，1974年
西班牙文版，巴塞隆納市基利出版社，1979年
印尼文版，班東比納迪出版社，1986年

色彩設計原理　英文版，紐約雷恩浩特出版社，1987年
增訂英文版，紐約韋利出版社，1998年

中國山水畫道　英文版，紐約麥格羅希爾出版社，1991年

設計與造形原理　英文版，紐約雷恩浩特出版社，1993年
英文版，紐約韋利出版社，1998年
西班牙文版，巴塞隆納基利出版社，1998年

電腦視覺設計　英文版，紐約利安波福出版社，1994年
增訂英文版，紐約諾頓出版社，2001年

INDEX OF WORKS

作品索引

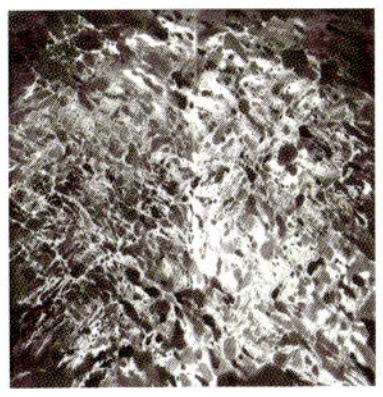

Sky And Land Expression #5
天地情之五（二連屏）
Ink,Watercolour and Acrylic on Cotton Fabric
200 x 200 cm [Diptych]
2008
Page.11

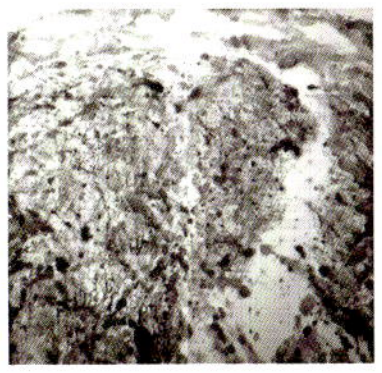

City Dream #12
城夢十二（二連屏）
Ink,Watercolour and Acrylic on Paper
176 x 190 cm [Diptych]
2004
Page.13

City Dream #9
城夢之九
Ink,Watercolour and Acrylic on Paper
157.5 x 96.5 cm, 2004
Page.15

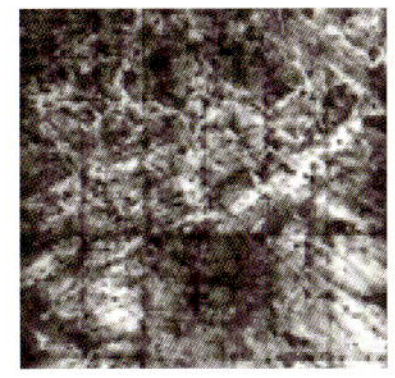

City Dream #6
城夢之六
Ink,Watercolour and Acrylic on Paper
217 x 99 cm, 2003
Page.17

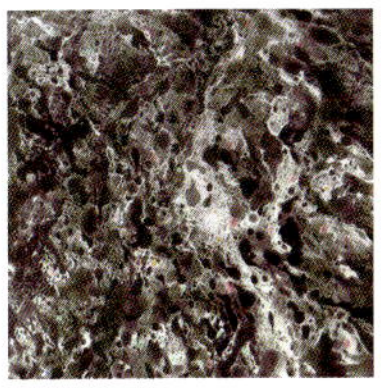

Flowing Water #4
流水之四
Ink,Watercolour and Acrylic on Paper
98 x 98 cm, 2007
Page.18

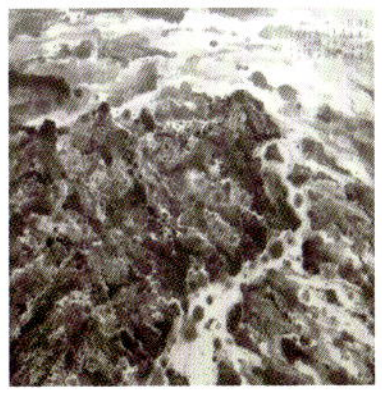

Great River #6
大江之六
Ink,Watercolour and Acrylic on Paper
116 x 117 cm [Diptych]
2004
Page.19

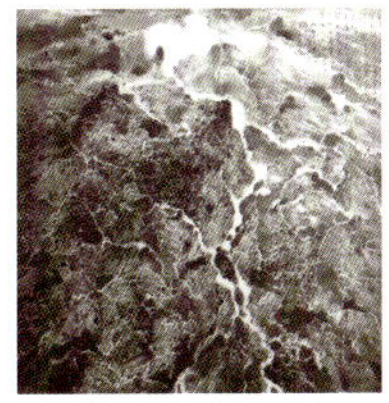

Mountain Clouds #4
山雲之四
Ink,Watercolour and Acrylic on Paper
97.5 x 95.5 cm, 2004
Page.20

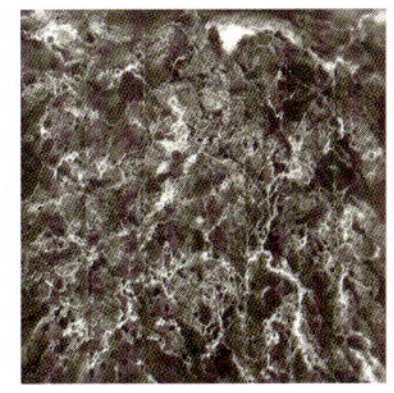

Deep In The Mountains #4
深山之四
Ink,Watercolour and Acrylic on Paper
68.5 x 68.5 cm, 2005
Page.21

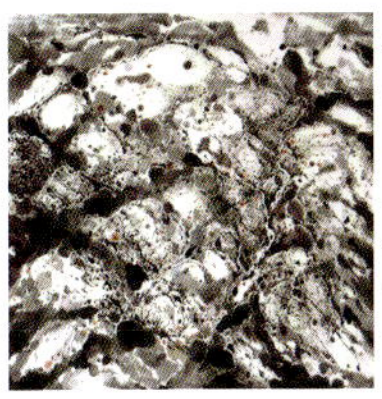

Autumn Mountain
秋山
Ink,Watercolour and Acrylic on Paper
66 x 66 cm
2006
Pg.22

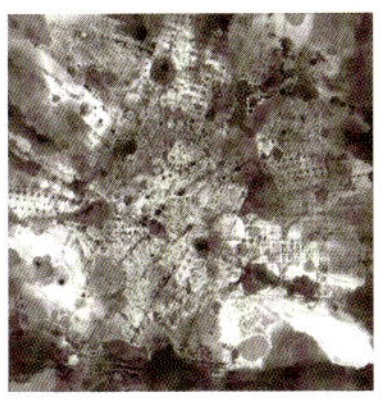

Dinghai Experiment #13
丁亥小品十三
Ink,Watercolour and Acrylic on Paper
32 x 32 cm
2007
Page.23

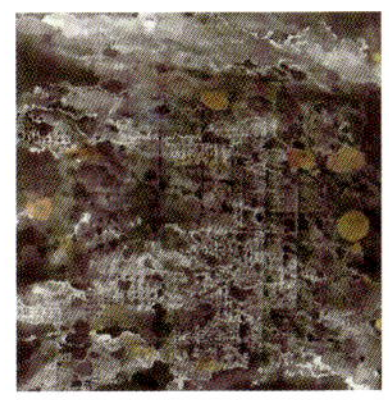

Dinghai Experiment #14
丁亥小品十四
Ink,Watercolour and Acrylic on Paper
32 x 32 cm, 2007
Page.24

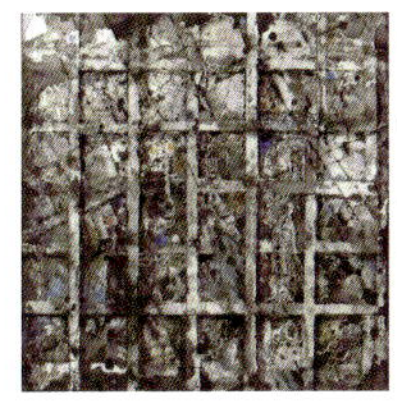

Dinghai Experiment#15
丁亥小品十五，
Ink,Watercolour and Acrylic on Paper
32 x 32 cm, 2007
Page.25

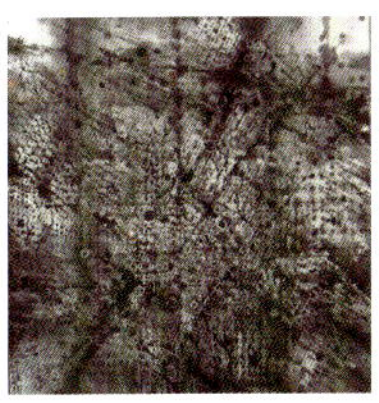

Dinghai Experiment#16
丁亥小品十六
Ink,Watercolour and Acrylic on Paper
32 x 32 cm, 2007
Page.26

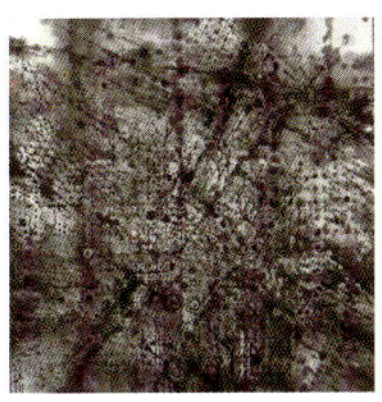

Dinghai Experiment #17
丁亥小品十七
Ink,Watercolour and Acrylic on Paper
32 x 32 cm, 2007
Page.27

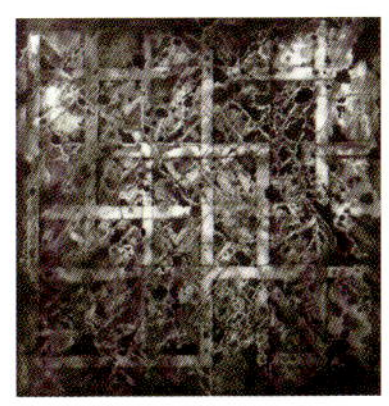

Dinghai Experiment #18
丁亥小品十八
Ink,Watercolour and Acrylic on Paper
32 x 32 cm, 2007
Page.28

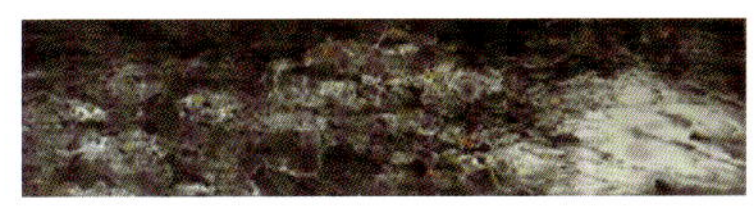

Edge Of Sea
海緣
Ink,Watercolour and Acrylic on Paper
33.5 x 135 cm, 2007
Page.29

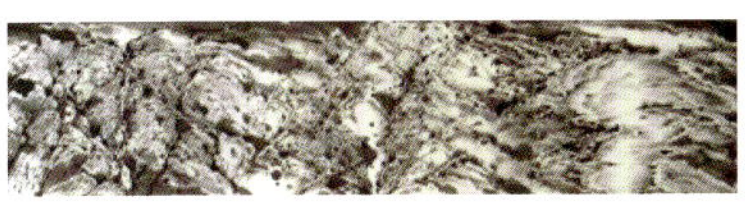

Linked landscape #1
連景之一
Ink,Watercolour and Acrylic on Paper
17 x 70.5 cm, 2007
Page.30

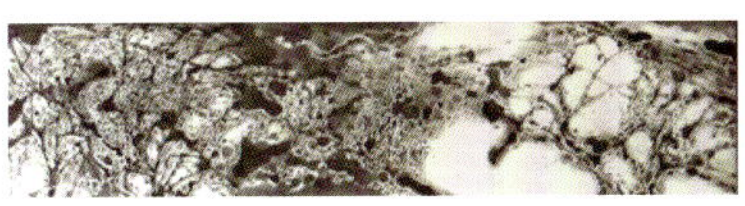

Linked landscape #2
連景之二
Ink,Watercolour and Acrylic on Paper
17 x 70.5 cm, 2007
Page.31

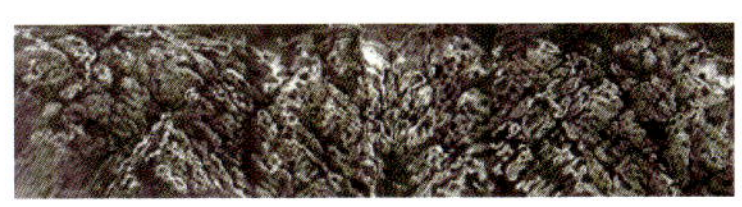

Linked landscape #3
連景之三
Ink,Watercolour and Acrylic on Paper
16.5 x 70 cm, 2007
Page.32

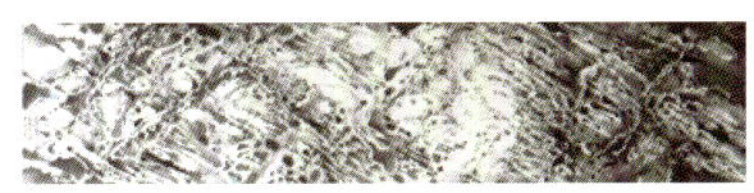

Linked landscape #4
連景之四
Ink,Watercolour and Acrylic on Paper
15.5 x 70.5 cm, 2007
Page.33

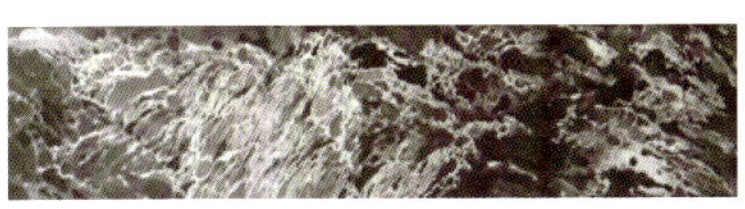

Linked landscape #5
連景之五
Ink,Watercolour and Acrylic on Paper
15.5 x 70 cm, 2007
Page.34

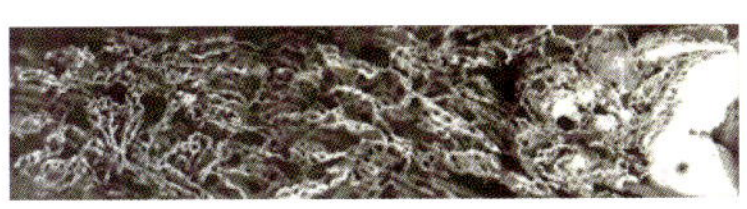

Linked landscape #6
連景之六
Ink,Watercolour and Acrylic on Paper
16.5 x 70 cm, 2007
Page.35

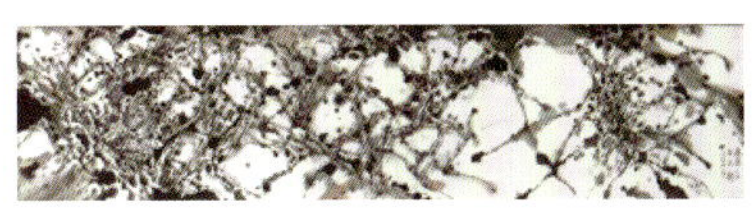

Linked landscape #7
連景之七
Ink,Watercolour and Acrylic on Paper
16 x 70 cm, 2007
Page.36

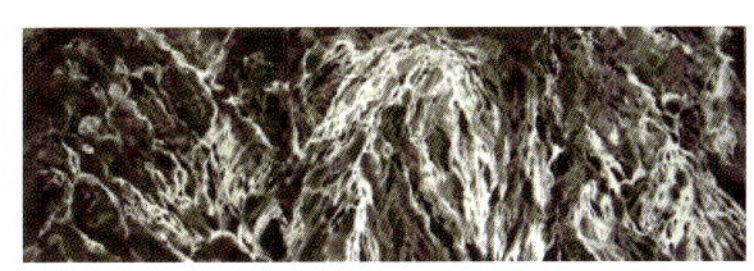

Running Water Forever #2
水長流之二
Ink,Watercolour and Acrylic on Paper
46 x 143.5 cm, 2007
Page.37

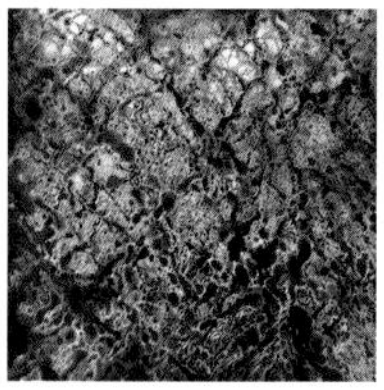

Spreading The Roots #3
展根之三
Ink,Watercolour and Acrylic on Paper
80 x 81 cm, 2007
Page.39

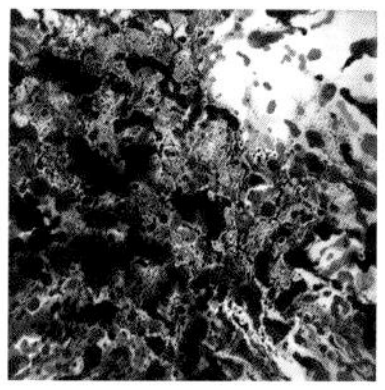

Spreading The Roots #4
展根之四
Ink,Watercolour and Acrylic on Paper
87.5 x 87.5 cm, 2007
Page.40

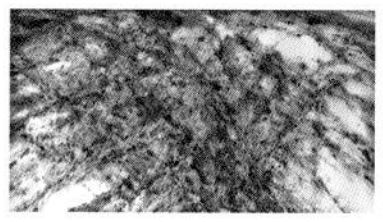

Spreading The Roots #5
展根之五
Ink,Watercolour and Acrylic on Paper
95 x 177 cm, 2007
Page.41

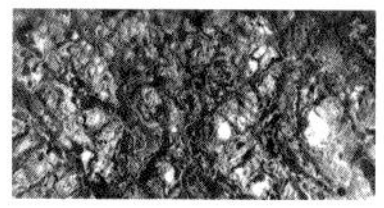

Spreading The Roots #6
展根之六
Ink,Watercolour and Acrylic on Paper
68.5 x 138.5 cm, 2008
Page.45

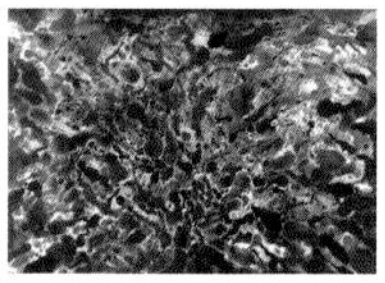

Spreading The Roots #8
展根之八
Ink,Watercolour and Acrylic on Paper
64 x 91.5 cm, 2008
Page.46

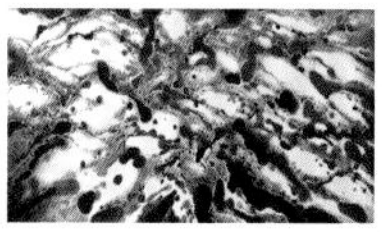

Deep In The Mountains #11
深山十一
IInk,Watercolour and Acrylic on Paper
67 x 117.5 cm, 2008
Page.47

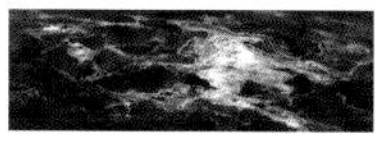

Edge Of Sea #2
海緣之二
Ink,Watercolour and Acrylic on Paper
30.5 x 94.5 cm, 2008
Page.48

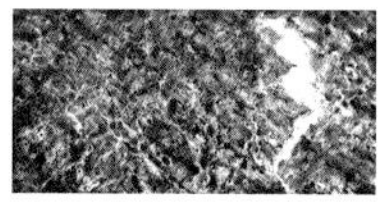

Autumn River
秋江
Ink,Watercolour and Acrylic on Paper
68.5 x 138.5 cm, 2008
Page.49

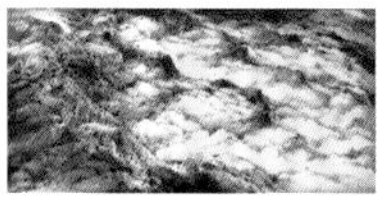

Mountain Clouds #5
山雲之五
Ink,Watercolour and Acrylic on Paper
61 x 123 cm, 2008
Page.51

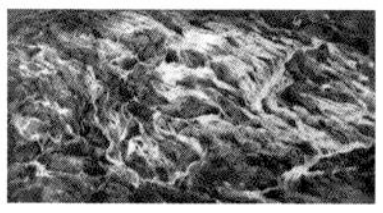

Running Water Forever #5
水長流之五
Ink,Watercolour and Acrylic on Paper
61 x 123 cm, 2008
Page.53

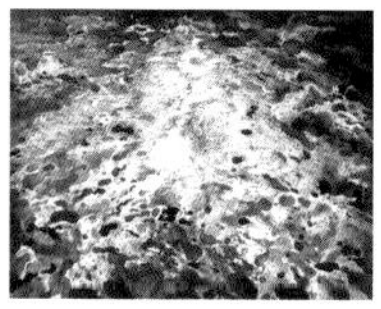

Water Melody #3
水韻之三
Ink,Watercolour and Acrylic on Paper
95 x 123 cm, 2008
Page.55

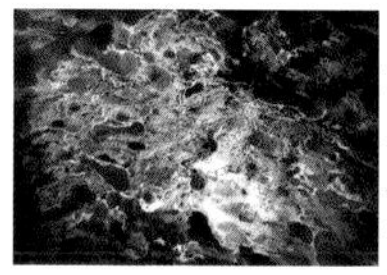

Water Melody #5
水韻之五
Ink,Watercolour and Acrylic on Paper
84 x 123 cm, 2008
Page.56

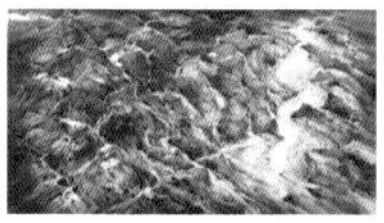

Great River #15
大江十五
Ink,Watercolour and Acrylic on Paper
95 x 176 cm, 2008
Page.57

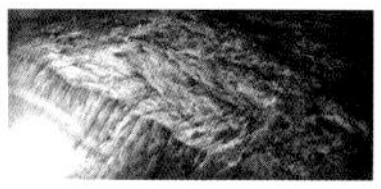

Meditation #26
澄懷廿六
Ink,Watercolour and Acrylic on Paper
96.5 x 212 cm, 2008
Page.61